Anna Maria Venturini

A Fearless Italian Adventurer

by Alice (Allyson) Hansen

Copyright

Editing and Cover Design by: Paula F. Howard at
paula@aHowardActivity.com

Interior Design by: Linda Hurley at
ImpressionsBookDesignServices.com

ISBN: 979-8-9852263-6-2

PRINTED IN THE UNITED STATES OF AMERICA
AHA! A HOWARD ACTIVITY PUBLICATION

More copies may be ordered online at Amazon.com
or through https://www.TheWritersMall.com

Map of Friuli Venezia Giulia
Northeastern Italy

Dedication

To Anna Maria and her gracious Italian friends.
Thanks for the memories.

Anna at three years old

My First photo
Visco, Italy 1925

Here is the first photo my parents ever took of me. They waited until I was three to take this picture because, before that, I had very little hair, and I was not a pretty baby. I was small for my age but very active and started walking when I was seven months old. By the time this photo was taken, I had invented several new dances and enjoyed entertaining. I had a strong will to make my own way in the world.

To take this photo, my parents had to promise me chocolates and goodies. I kept running away because the photographer scared me. He hid behind the camera under a big black rug. It was hard for me to stand still for very how long; so, to encourage me, my parents let me hold my parasol. As you can see in this picture, I was still suspicious of the photographer and would not smile for him.

Foreword

I was born in 1922, the same year Mussolini declared himself dictator of Italy. My middle-aged parents both suffered greatly during WWI, and when I was born, I represented a new beginning for them.

Here is the story of my life, woven into the complex and ever-changing military history of the northeastern Italian province of Friuli, Venezia Giulia. Here is also the story of how my life was linked to the establishment of the United States Air Force Base in Aviano, Italy, where I worked for over twenty years. I took the Air Force motto of "Aim High" to heart.

I want to thank all those people I met while working for the Allied Forces in Italy. I especially want to thank my wonderful friends from Aviano AFB who made my work so pleasant and who left me with my dearest memories. To my dear friend, Allyson, thank you for helping me assemble this book.

Ciao, my dear friends. My thoughts will always be on your wings, and maybe we will meet again in another place and another time.

Chapter 1
Anna's Mother Ida Mlaker Schubert

*I*t *was an unusually cold and windy morning* on February 2, 1879, when the seventh child to Ignaz Mlaker and Margherita Kolbic, Ida, was born in Trieste, Austria, on the coast of the Adriatic Sea. They found Ida to be a lovely, intelligent child who later went to the finest schools in Trieste.

Four decades later, Ida would give birth to "Anna." This is Anna's story. But first, let us meet her mother… Ida Mlaker.

The Mlaker family members were aristocratic and well-educated with high social standing in the city of Trieste. The city had thrived under Austrian rule and had grown to be a great modern cosmopolitan city as Austria's only seaport. When Ida was young, the family moved to Ljubljana, Austria, after her father became a trainmaster there.

When her family eventually returned to Trieste, Ida was a young woman and found employment as a postmistress for the Austrian government after her graduation. At the age of eighteen, Ida fell in love with Adolfo Schubert, a government employee with the police force. He was a widower and twenty-two years her senior, but well-educated and from a wealthy family, therefore, age was less of a restriction. After a brief courtship, they were married and by the following year, Ida was expecting their first child.

Mlaker family in the garden at Via Trenovia, Trieste
Left to right back row: Ida, Carlo, Margharita, Giuseppi
Seated from left: Gilda, Margharita Kolbic (Ida's mother), Paola, and Ignaz (Ida's father)

When Adolfo decided to retire, he moved the family northwest of Trieste to a small farm in the country on the outskirts of Visco, Austria, a small village forty-five kilometers from Trieste. The nearest town was Palmanova some five kilometers further west of Visco and just across the Italian border. The dirt road in front of their house led to Gorizia, so their new address became Via Gorizia, Number 4.

The farmhouse was constructed of concrete blocks and trimmed with beautiful moldings and fine woodwork. It was made even more attractive by ornamental pine trees and bushes which Adolfo planted to frame the house. A wrought iron fence with a decorated gate enclosed several well-defined flower and vegetable gardens. They had two fine carriage horses and another one for riding.

Home built by Alfonso and Ida on via Gorizia No. 4 in Visco
with four-year-old Anna standing by the gate
1926

Adolfo was kindhearted and generous, and the people in Visco demonstrated affection and respect for the entire family which grew with the addition of his four sons. Their first son, Adolfo (Dolfi) was born in 1901. Eight years later, their second son, Fedrico was born. In 1912, their third son, Piero (Picko) came along just two years before their last son, Guido, arrived in 1914. After Guido was born, Dolfi, their eldest, left home at age thirteen to live with his maternal grandparents in Trieste and attend private school.

Ida loved being a mother and caring for her children and spent most of her free time with them. She enjoyed sewing, knitting, and crocheting while sitting in the wooden window seat Adolfo had made for her. Her sisters, Margherita (Yetta), and Paola, frequently visited them from Trieste. They were welcome guests who came often for extended stays bringing along other family members and friends. Adolfo and Ida also enjoyed frequent visits to Trieste and to Gorizia.

*Ida's brother, Giuseppi, and
sisters Margherita (Jetti) and Paola*

Ida Mlaker

Because of her experience at the post office in Trieste, Ida was hired as the local postmistress of Visco. She had a working knowledge of several languages which helped her not only with local mail, but also with commercial mailings and correspondences from the Austrian German states: Austria, Poland, Czechoslovakia, Bulgaria, Hungary, Romania, and Serbia. Working as the postmistress wasn't the only thing that set Ida apart from other local women in Visco, she also had a housekeeper to help run her household and do most of the cooking. To Ida, this was not unusual, since she had grown up with servants, nor did she like doing housework. The local villagers admired her intellect even though they could not identify with Ida's modern cosmopolitan lifestyle.

Adolfo was a gentleman farmer and hired other locals to do most of the hard labor on the farm, while he enjoyed horseback riding and entertaining friends and relatives. He greatly enjoyed the quiet country life and occupied himself with light gardening and small tasks around the farm. However, this peaceful, loving existence that Ida and Adolfo shared, abruptly came to an end with the beginning of World War I.

When the Austrian line was broken west of them at River Piave, Italian, British, and American troops swept eastward throughout the area. City officials and Austrian government employees were suspect and sent to detention camps in southern Italy for the duration of the war. All those who were sympathetic to Austria were displaced, including the local priest. The order came for them to pack only one suitcase. Ida and Adolfo found it difficult to determine what to pack because of the uncertainly of where they were going and for how long they would be gone.

Before they boarded the train to leave, Ida and the boys were separated from Adolfo. Government escorts took Adolfo to the train station where he was sent to Sicily along with all the men from the community who were bound together, making it most uncomfortable. Adolfo was tall, but he was tied to the priest who was a short man. The size difference made Adolfo slump over to make the priest more comfortable. Everyone on the train was without food, water, or toilets for over twenty hours. The cattle cars used to transport them were cold and drafty; by the time Adolfo arrived at the detention center, he was suffering with pneumonia.

Ida, Fedrico, Piero and Guido were sent by boxcar to San Severino in the Le Marche region, west of Ancona, Italy. They rode the train trip standing up and in a boxcar without heat. Some people huddled together, putting children in the middle to try and keep them warm.

Before the journey's end, many people had collapsed onto the floor. Those with food were kind enough to share it with the children. Ida was still breastfeeding Guido, now nearly a year old. He became ill during the trip, running a high fever, and began to cry and sweat as a result. By the time Ida could find medical care for him, he was diagnosed with meningitis. The doctor told Ida that Guido would not live beyond a week, so she attended him constantly, but because of her own lack of food, could not produce enough milk for him. Even though he lived, his brain had been permanently damaged, and she realized he would need special care throughout his life.

The detainees begged authorities to give them milk for their children and, finally, after six months, they were given a milk cow for several families to share. Poverty was rampant throughout Italy by now, and most people were slowly starving. They dug roots and picked grass and leaves, turning them into salads and drinks.

When Adolfo became so ill the guards were sure he would die anyway, they released him from the detention camp in Sicily and shipped him north to be with Ida and their sons. But shortly after the family was reunited, Adolfo passed away.

Ida was devastated but hid her grief for the sake of the children. There were several other Austrian women and children from Gorizia and Trieste, who were also placed with Italian families in the area. Sometimes they had small gatherings so their children could play while the women visited and spoke German to each other. However, these gatherings were closely supervised, and they were watched by local police.

One way Ida earned money was to meet with other women to sew, knit, and crochet for people who were willing to pay. Her work was so fine and delicate, wealthy people would hire her to put lace on their dresses and scarves. She was even hired by one lady to make lace for her daughter's doll clothes. Ida was later placed with an Italian family and received a small pension from the Italian government to help care for her children. She and her sons stayed for three years in San Severino before being released and allowed to go back home to Visco. By that time, the Austrian border had been moved eastward beyond Gorizia, now making Visco a part of Italy.

Upon returning home, Ida found that their home had been broken into and ransacked. Many things had been stolen or destroyed. The house had been degraded with trash and garbage left in heaps throughout the house and what little clothing had been left in the house was found dirty and on the floor. Ida's lace curtains and beautiful tablecloths, which she had brought from Trieste when she married, were now destroyed, or missing. Several of her large oriental rugs had been stolen, and there was dirt, leaves, and mud tracked throughout the house.

When she entered the kitchen, she noticed her large German cook stove, built into the wall, was destroyed and parts of it were missing. The bricks around the foundation of the stove had also been stolen and most of the chimney bricks were pulled from the wall. Pots and pans were missing, as were most of her kitchen utensils, including her good butcher knives made of German steel. There were a few mismatched pieces of china and ceramic dishes scattered on the counter tops and floor. The kitchen table and chairs were gone from the house, but later she found one broken chair lying in the back yard. The beautiful antique hope chests from Ida's family were gone, along with several large paintings and an expensive wall clock. Her library shelves had been emptied of books, papers, and maps, all of which had been in her family for many years. She was heartbroken.

Upstairs in her bedroom, she found most of her expensive clothes had also been ruined or stolen, even her fine silk scarves, or silk undergarments, had not been spared. What was left of her hats and purses were scattered or dirty, and all her shoes, gloves, and fur coats were missing.

The gardens and orchards around the house were overrun with weeds and brush. Shutters on the house had been damaged or broken, and the walls needed to be repaired and painted. She was grateful when some of the local farmers came by to help cut the grass and trim the shrubs.

After a few weeks, a small Italian cook stove was dropped off during the night in her front yard. Little by little, more of her household items began to be returned by others. The local people began explaining why they had taken her things.

"We wanted to 'protect' them against theft by soldiers or gypsies," some said. "We saved them for your return." Several large carpets were also returned. Ida's family in Trieste offered their support and helped her refurnish the house. With a quiet strength, she began to rebuild her life.

Perhaps most importantly, the position as postmistress, which she had held for the Austrian government before the war, was offered to her again, this time by the Italian government. So, again, she became the postmistress at Visco and for the surrounding area. She converted her parlor into the new post office and

Ida Mlaker's Postmistress desk

planted a small flower garden in front of the house. As people passed by or came to pick up their mail at her parlor window, they would comment on how pretty her flowers looked. Sometimes people stopped by just to talk and see how she was dressed. She was known for wearing tailored suits and colorful clothes with nice hats while she worked.

After the war ended, a few rich Italian families returned to their villas in the region from Tuscany and Umbria. These families were often persistent and demanded extra consideration and services from the post office that Ida did not normally provide as a government employee. They often wanted Ida to translate correspondence in different languages and help them write personal letters. Ida was always polite, discrete, and helpful whenever possible. She treated everyone with respect and did not accuse or judge anyone; therefore, the locals regarded her with respect and admiration. Over time, she resolved her anger about having lost most of her family heirlooms, she realized so many other people had also suffered great losses during the war. With that in mind, she forgave them all.

Ida was now an attractive forty-one-year-old widow with four children. She had a good complexion and kept a fine figure. Her clothing was tailored, and she wore stylish heeled shoes. She enjoyed traveling to Trieste often to visit relatives. Despite everything she had experienced during the war, and afterwards, Ida had felt optimistic about the future.

Chapter 2
Anna's Father, Giuseppe Venturini

Giuseppe (Pepi) Venturini, Anna's father, was born in his parents' home in Visco, Austria, on August 8, 1876. His extended family shared a large farmhouse and worked the family-owned farm. From an early age, Pepi was expected to do farm chores and was a hard worker. He was even-tempered and showed a great deal of common sense.

In school, he excelled in reading, math, and German, but after elementary school, he was self-taught through experimentation and experience and was blessed with an excellent memory. By the time he was twelve, Pepi had already read many books on science and history. He also spoke an Italian dialect known as *Friulano,* a quick, witty dialect of Latin with many borrowed words and sounds from the German and Slavic languages. It was only spoken or understood in the northeastern region of Italy known as Friuli.

As a young man, Pepi dreamed of traveling. When he tried to enlist in the Austrian army in 1911, they rejected him for having a thin bone structure, so his sense of adventure took him to the shipyards in Naples. There he found a job managing the food store on a passenger ship bound for the United States. The ship took two weeks to cross the Atlantic, docking at New York City Harbor. After a short stay in New York, he would work on the return trip to Naples. During these trips, he met interesting people and enjoyed discussing history and world affairs with both passengers and crew. As an outgoing, friendly person, he was quick to pick up phrases in different languages. He enjoyed being on the move and working for the shipping company, but after several years, the excitement wore off and the job became routine. He felt an urge to settle down and decided to return to Visco and the countryside where he was born.

Back on the farm, he began helping his brother; then later, established a food cooperative in Visco. All went well, and he ran a successful business until he was called upon to join the Austrian army. By this time, the Austrians needed more troops, and had become less selective than the first time he had tried to enlist. After being accepted, he sold his business and was sent to Innsbruck, Austria.

As the war progressed, Pepi, and other soldiers, began expressing doubt that Austria was on the winning side of the war. One day, the son of a wealthy local man overheard Pepi discussing the topic and reported him to authorities as a traitor to Austria. Because Pepi was well-liked and a natural leader, the commander was afraid that Pepi's talk about Austria possibly losing the war, would lower morale among the other soldiers, so to set an example, the commander ordered Pepi to be arrested. He was put on trial and the court-marshal ended in a death sentence which was to be carried out within the week.

Another Colonel, however, decided Pepi should be sent to the Russian front with only a bayonet, hoping he would stop a bullet intended for another Austrian soldier. On three separate occasions, Pepi fought bravely without being wounded. Each time, he cleverly found discarded rifles and distinguished himself as an excellent marksman. The last time at the Russian Front, the battle lasted so long, and he fought so hard, that he fell into a ditch exhausted, unable to move. When the Russians found him alive, they took him prisoner and sent him by train to a prison war camp in Russia.

Upon arriving at the prison camp, Pepi saw how poor and miserable conditions were for the prisoners. Many were dying of starvation and dysentery. He volunteered to manage the food stores and kitchen, and, because of his background, he was granted the job. Even though he was a prisoner, he maintained a good attitude and soon learned enough Russian to impress some of the officers.

One day, while riding a horse to deliver water and supplies to the other end of camp, he caught the eye of a Russian colonel. Pepi was a good horseman and impressed the colonel enough to be asked to manage the colonel's private stables outside the camp.

Later, after working in the stables for a brief time, Pepi became the personal driver for the colonel's family. He accompanied the colonel's wife and children each time they needed to use the carriage or to go to the market. The colonel and his wife knew many of the Russian officers and had some wealthy friends. When anyone came to visit, Pepi would also care for their horses. His pleasant personality and positive attitude gained him genuine affection and respect.

Pepi continued improving his knowledge of the Russian language and was often invited into intellectual conversations. He learned how to navigate high society and conducted himself in a refined and polite manner. It was in this fortunate setting that he outlived the dangers of World War I.

In 1917, at the end of the war, most prisoners had no money for train fare and had to walk home or work their way home. Many times, they needed to beg for food and shelter along the way, which resulted in some prisoners taking up to two years to make the journey home. But Pepi was given the fare to travel home to Visco by train because he had been an officer's aid. At the train station in Vienna, Lenin greeted all prisoners with a handshake as they left.

Returning home to the old farmhouse in Visco, Pepi entertained everyone with his wartime adventure stories. He worked on the farm with his brother, but after a while, he became restless again. He missed the intellectual discussions and camaraderie he had experienced with the upper class during the war. He also longed to establish himself and have a family of his own, and he began taking long horseback rides throughout the countryside contemplating his future.

One day while riding his horse to Visco, he encountered Ida Schubert walking along the roadside. Upon seeing her, he slowed his horse to study her. She was wearing a tailored suit and modern hat to match. Her shoes had short heels, which she placed slowly and carefully as she walked in a poised and erect manner. He observed that she was completely different from local farm women who wore loose clothing and dark scarves pulled over their heads, and men's boots or clogs.

As he rode past, he greeted her and smiled. She returned his greeting but continued to look straight ahead. With a tip of his hat, he rode on, but not before she had made an intriguing impression on him.

After several inquiries, he learned she was a widow and had recently returned from a detention camp in Le Marche with her three sons. He also learned she was the postmistress, so he made a point to stop by and engage her in conversation. He had always wanted a German-speaking wife and felt affection for her immediately after their first conversation.

When he saw that her house and farm needed work, he offered to help her. He also noticed that her sons were growing up and out of her control, doing little to help her run the farm. He began to care for her, and his love grew quickly. He was convinced he could help her make a fresh start and put the despair of the war years behind her. In those days it was uncommon for people of their age to get married. But Pepi pursued her until she finally agreed. They felt shy about their situation and wanted to be married quietly, so early one morning, at six a.m., they were married in the Visco chapel just before Mass. Only the priest and Ida's housekeeper were there to witness their marriage.

After receiving the news that Ida and Pepi were already married, Ida's sisters came to visit. They were disappointed that Ida had married Pepi so quickly without a chance for them to know him before the marriage took place. They considered Pepi inferior in social status and education and thought he was not good enough for Ida, but she continued to defend him. Ida's family, though polite, never accepted him wholeheartedly. Several years later, however, they began to appreciate him because he was hard-working, honest, and did not speak like a common farmer. His worldly intellectualism began to win them over and they found he could discuss current events from an interesting, confident perspective.

Energized by his love for Ida, Pepi took responsibility for restoring the house and farm seriously and was dedicated to Ida and his new family. But Fedrico, twelve at the time, and Piero, who was nine, did not accept Pepi as an authoritative father figure. They continued to mourn the loss of their own father and refused to cooperate with Pepi. The boys manipulated Ida through her own grief and created continuous trouble around the house.

Guido, on the other hand, only seven, enjoyed having a new father and followed Pepi around the farm. He was still unable to talk but smiled often, and respected Pepi. Ida admired Pepi for his dedication to her and the farm and depended upon him for support and companionship.

The following year after their marriage, Ida became pregnant with the child who would be named Anna Maria. She was born from her parents' love and respect for each other which continued to grow through their years together.

Ida and Giuseppi (Pepi)
Anna's parents on their wedding day

Chapter 3
Anna's Early Childhood

Visco, Italy

*A*nna *Maria Venturini was born in her parent's bedroom* at four in the morning on Thursday, June 5, 1922. Her parents felt blessed and delighted to have a daughter. It would be another three years before Ida would retire from the post office and devote nearly all her time to Anna's welfare and happiness.

Ida made beautiful linens and trimmed them with lace for Anna's little iron-framed bed which was painted white and trimmed with roses and angels. The sides of her bed had panels of netting to protect her from falling out. It was placed against the wall near her mother's side of the bed in her parent's room, and as Anna grew older, she often climbed out and into her parent's big bed to cuddle next to her mother.

Anna's early years were full of freedom and happiness. In good weather, she was irresistibly drawn outside into nature and preferred running barefoot. By the time she was four, she and her older brother, Guido, were about the same age developmentally and became good playmates. He began speaking small words around the same time Anna was learning to make full sentences. They often packed up her dolls and took them on little excursions, dressing them up and acting out scenes of plays she created Ida would make boiled or baked apples and sprinkle sugar on top as an added treat, for them to take along. Sometimes she gave them sweet, dried pumpkin slices. She also made corn-on-a-stick, which was another one of their favorite treats. The children would carry the corn cobs around the courtyard, chewing and sucking on the sweet corn juice throughout the afternoon.

As she grew, Anna filled her days by letting her imagination run free. Still too young to go to school, she entertained herself by sitting on the window seat facing the road or hiding somewhere to watch people pass by. She would call out to school children walking past, sometimes hiding behind the fence or a bush only to jump out, laughing to surprise them. Sometimes, she climbed high into a tree and pretended to be a bird to catch their attention.

Each day the children made a game of looking for Anna because they were never sure where she would be hiding. There were two walnut trees in her yard, and when in season, the children would help her pick nuts off the ground in exchange for a few to take home. She often invited them into the garden to sit in the front yard gazebo or to play on her swing. Hours were spent on the swing since swinging was her favorite pastime. Feeling the wind on her face and ruffling her hair made her imagine she was flying like Charles Lindberg, the aviator. When she was older, she loved making trips to the local villages and farms by bike to feel the wind and to soothe her adventurous spirit.

In her bedroom were windows low enough that she could lie in bed and still see outside. She would study the sky and ever-changing clouds. Many kinds of birds came to rest on the garden gate and fence around her house. When disturbed, the birds would fly into the trees near Anna's upstairs window. As she watched them disappear and scatter in the wind, she wished to fly as quickly as they did into the sky. She studied them at great length, calling out to them in bird languages she invented. Her beautiful white frilly curtains were delicate enough to allow her to look through them to see the birds, while they could not see her making their sounds, this amused Anna. There were also wisteria vines running along the iron fence, which gave off a delightful scent when in bloom. Each morning upon awakening, she would go to the window and look out, dreaming about all the possibilities awaiting her. She was enjoying the freedom of her childhood.

On many occasions, she was awakened by the sound of honking geese. She knew they were being herded through the early morning mist by two young sisters who lived on a nearby farm. Each morning, the girls drove their geese around the countryside to comb the fields for snails or grain dropped during the harvest. These girls were from a poor family and needed to conserve every bit of grain they could find. They dutifully collected handfuls of wheat which they found left in the fields. They wrapped the wheat stalks into little bundles with string and slung them over their shoulders like fuzzy backpacks. Sometimes, Anna wondered if her father deliberately left small piles of wheat along the edges for them to find.

***

Most everyone was poor in Italy during this period after the war, all necessities had to be conserved and used wisely. Anna's family was considered well off compared to others in the area, because they had plenty of fresh meat and produce from the farm. Also, her mother received a rather large pension from having worked as a government employee during the previous years.

On Monday mornings, Anna would accompany her mother, Ida, to Piazza Grande in Palmanova to the market. It was only five kilometers away and they enjoyed walking and talking together. Her mother never rode a bike in those days, because a mature, upper-class lady did not ride a bicycle. From the time Anna was six, she rode her bike to the market in Palmanova by herself, sometimes taking the long way home. She was small for her age and when she went shopping, she was so short that when she stood at the counter, the other ladies looked over her head and tried to crowd in front of her. But Anna would have none of it.

"Excuse me, but I'm next!" she would call up to them. Looking down, the ladies were surprised to see such a strong voice coming from such a little person. Her determination made them step back and laugh. She often got attention for the outfits she wore, especially in the sweltering summer when she wore a beret and sunglasses. It was rare to see anyone wearing sunglasses in those days, except at beach resorts. But Anna never was just "anyone."

***

During those days, there were not enough people in Visco to support a regular market day. But there was a convenience store where sugar, raisins, tobacco, and a few mints in a jar were sold. The town also had a drug store that sold medicines and spices, and a baker who sold loaves of bread. Visco also had a butcher shop in town, but it was widely believed the scales were not adjusted properly. Many felt they had been taken advantage of and suspected the owner of the shop of cheating the especially targeted poor and the elderly. Some people even claimed the butcher sold old meat covered in spices to disguise a tainted flavor. He became so unpopular that after a few years, he was forced to close his shop and left town.

Another custom the local farmers had was to set up little carts and sell eggs, milk, fruit, and vegetables when in season. One farmer's wife loaded a basket of eggs each day and walked many kilometers, selling eggs until her basket was empty. Sometimes she would trade one egg for a small amount of sugar. Chocolates and sweets were not sold anywhere near the village, so Anna's aunts sent chocolates and goodies from Trieste by bus to Palmanova where the family could pick them up.

There was a man from Chioggia, near Venice, who often sold onions by bike. The tops were braided, and Anna's mother bought several bunches of them each fall, which lasted through the entire winter. Another traveling salesman came from Grado, selling fresh fish from a big wooden box filled with ice. Ann's mother bought fish once or twice a week and sometimes made a fish sauce called brodetto which Anna dearly loved.

Most farmers in the area kept pigs, poultry, and rabbits for their own consumption. Pepi and Ida kept several pigs of their own. A local farmer who butchered animals would come by each fall to kill and cut up the hogs. Then he and Pepi would make sausages, cut hams and slabs of bacon that Pepi would later smoke and store in the cellar. Anna's family also raised chickens, which scratched and pecked their way around the courtyard.

There were always several cats sunning themselves around the garden and in the windowsills. Anna liked to dress them in her doll clothes and carry them around like babies to everyone's amusement. There was one cat named Matisse which she dearly loved. The first time Anna experienced grief was when Matisse was bitten by a poisonous lizard, and later died. Not even the vet could help keep her cat alive, and her whole family mourned the loss with her.

***

Anna's father, Pepi, had a fine riding horse which he rode for pleasure. Occasionally, he would let Anna and Guido ride his horse around the courtyard. They, also, had a muscular workhorse to do heavier farm work, and pull the farm cart. Anna loved animals and had a little lamb that was tame enough to ride on. She fed it handpicked bouquets of flowers and clover and dressed it with hats and scarves then led it around the courtyard to entertain her family and friends. Sometimes, Anna would hook a small wagon behind her dog and load it up with dolls and bedding, then have the dog pull them around for the neighbors to see. There was always something fun to do with the animals and she loved inventing ways to get attention and praise.

***

Life was quiet and peaceful in the country, except for an occasional airplane flying overhead. When Anna heard the plane, she would study the sky and dream of becoming a pilot one day.

The roads around Visco and in front of her house were not paved yet, and a local veterinarian was the only one in the area with a car. Most people walked or rode bikes past Anna's house, except for an occasional farm wagon or cart pulled by horses or oxen. Anna was often entertained by watching people as they passed by. Occasionally, a nice carriage would travel passed creating a sensation; everyone strained to see who was in the carriage and, most importantly, how they were dressed.

Anna loved traveling to Trieste with her mother. Pepi would hire a local farmer who ran a taxi service with a single horse and buggy to take them as far as the train station in Sagrado about fifteen kilometers away. From the Sagrado train station, connections could be made to all major cities. Anna was always excited about visiting her aunts in Trieste. They lived in fine homes and often went to the exclusive tea and coffee houses in the city center to socialize. She enjoyed seeing store windows dressed in the latest fashions and styles. An abundance of chocolates and sweets were always beautifully displayed in pastry shop cases.

As a happy child, Anna always rewarded her aunts with sweet smiles and affection. They would encourage her to do little dances and entertain them with impromptu skits. She was outgoing and expressive and gained acceptance for almost anything she did. She could brighten anyone's day with a smile or a comic gesture, as if she was an adorable pet, herself, that everyone enjoyed and wanted to hug and touch. Her childhood had many happy moments like this.

Anna knew how to draw attention to herself wherever she went. On Sundays, when she attended church in Visco, people would watch for her to see what kind of outfit she was wearing. Stylish dressing became important to her.

When she was four years old, she remembered having shiny, black patent leather shoes with a strap across the top and a button to secure them onto her feet. Back then, her feet were so tiny they looked like doll shoes. One of her favorite outfits was to wear those shoes with white socks, a summer dress, and a straw-colored hat with red and blue flowers attached to the brim on the right side. In winter, she had an expensive handmade coat with a thick fur collar and little bonnet trimmed with fur to match. As she marched into church, she would often put her chin up to try and look serious and dignified. She enjoyed hearing the murmuring sound of the commotion she created.

As she grew older, Anna studied fashion magazines, cutting out pictures of outfits she liked. Her mother would then have these outfits made especially for her. Anna was the first girl in the area to wear slacks with tailored jackets. She loved the freedom of wearing slacks and began to wear them nearly every day around the farm and into town.

Many times, when Anna returned home after a day of exploring, her clothing would be dirty, torn or even full of burrs and thistles. Her mother would look at her disapprovingly but accepted the fact that Anna was an extremely adventurous and active child. Often, she traipsed dirt into the house, and her mother would scold her.

Anna with pet lamb
in the courtyard behind her house
1926

"It's not dirt at all, its stardust," Anna said with a smile. She was so cute it was hard for her mother to correct her. Most of the time Anna did what she pleased. If her parents tried to restrain her, she would pout or fuss until they gave in.

She had a mischievous streak and liked playing tricks on her parents, and brother, Guido. She would move or hide things from them and appear innocent when they became distressed about not finding them. Then, Anna would simply laugh and make the hidden items magically "reappear." Her parents soon caught on, but poor Guido never quite understood the little tricks she played on him.

Even the church was not spared her trickery. Anna sometimes invented elaborate stories to tell the priest during confession. However, the one thing she didn't confess was the fact that these stories were purely from her own imagination. It might have saved her some penances if she did them in the future.

Anna Maria and her childhood friend
Maria Pasqualis in Anna's backyard

Anna would often try to prove how brave she was by jumping from high places. Her parents would become angry and afraid she would hurt herself, however her friends seemed impressed. She did have one fear, however. She was afraid of storms. Thunder, lightning, or rainstorms with high winds frightened her the most. Perhaps because she couldn't control them.

As she grew older, Anna spent most mornings in the company of her mother. Ida would read to her and together, they would do small tasks around the house. While Ida cooked, Anna would read or look at pictures from books at the table. Her mother insisted that Anna study German for one hour each day and sometimes they sang German songs together. Something she always enjoyed very much.

Ida had a maid to help manage the house and prepare the midday and evening meals. In northern Italy, it was not customary for adults to eat breakfast. Usually, a cup of coffee and sometimes a piece of bread was all they had to start the day with. Children, on the other hand, usually had a light breakfast of bread soaked in milk and eaten in a bowl. Sometimes Ida would sprinkle sugar or cinnamon on top for Anna.

Pranzo (lunch), the largest meal of the day, was served around midday. This was Anna's favorite meal because the whole family sat together talking around the table. After pranzo, everyone took a short siesta before having a cup of coffee or hot tea, then returning to work around mid-afternoon. It would be suppertime, ora di cena, in the evening before the house was full of noise and conversation again.

In the afternoons, while her parents rested, Anna would take the opportunity to leave the house and freely explore the countryside. She was often gone for hours, sometimes not returning home until after dark. This distressed her mother. Ida often worried that her independent little girl would be kidnapped or hurt. She tried scaring Anna by telling her a band of traveling gypsies might steal her when seeing she was so tanned from being out in the sun and looking unkempt and wild. But Anna was so strong-willed and full of energy; her parents, being middle-aged, had a hard time keeping up with her.

As for Anna's relationship with her father, she was a little afraid of him. Even though Pepi never struck Anna, one mean look from him sent her into hiding. As she grew older, she noticed her father seemed to be raising his voice in the house more often. Sometimes, she would hear her mother crying, and suspected it was because of the constant trouble Pepi's stepsons, Fedrico and Piero, caused him.

Each time Pepi tried to enforce discipline, the boys refused to cooperate, and would not help him on the farm. When they complained to Ida, she suggested they cooperate with Pepi, but never insisted or interfered. The boys manipulated her feelings, and Pepi resented Ida for being too weak to stand up to them.

Guido, Fedrico, Piero, Ida, and Pepi with Anna
standing on the footstool her father made for her

Finally, Pepi and Ida decided to send Fedrico to a private boarding school in Gorizia. Piero went to a public agricultural school near Udine and lived with a family in Pozzuolo. Once they were gone, some measure of peace was restored in the house.

Now Pepi expanded the orchards and traded land with another farmer so he could have a field closer to home. He worked in the vineyard, which started to produce enough wine for the family's consumption. Throughout the summer, he planted wheat and made hay, and was constantly working on repairs. He constructed a large barn behind the house, which was connected to the main structure with a large storage shed. A second floor was built to store hay and grain, with one side left open for the air to circulate. He was certainly not afraid of hard work, especially if it would help his family.

Guido started elementary school in Visco but did not do well, so he was sent to a boarding school in Gradisca, near Gorizia, especially designed for children with learning disabilities. There he learned to write and read easy books and was happy most of the time, he grew up to be good-looking with dark brown hair and blue eyes.

After he became a young man, girls would smile and flirt with him until they realized that his mind was not stable. He was easily confused and sometimes became angry and destroyed things until his violent mood passed. Because of his early illnesses, he never understood the consequences of his behavior.

Chapter 4
First School Days

*I*n 1928, *on Anna's first day of school*, her brother, Piero, took her there riding on his shoulders. Three teachers taught about fifteen children per class. First grade was taught in a single room, but second and third grades were combined in another room, as was fourth and fifth grades. School started each day at 8:00 a.m. and went until noon. The children were free in the afternoons, and not given homework; so, for Anna, each afternoon was spent playing or exploring. She was an average student and enjoyed drawing pictures and interacting with the other children. All classes were taught in Italian, and Italian grammar was emphasized. Unfortunately, the first-grade teacher took a disliking to Anna because she was more Austrian than Italian and spoke in the Triestino dialect like her mother.

Each day Anna would make a fuss about getting dressed for school. The wool uniforms made her itch, and she felt that they were too large and made her look fat. Her mother became desperate while trying to dress her, and her father would yell at her to cooperate. Anna also hated the wool stockings because she thought they made her look ugly, and they felt too tight on her legs. Being used to running barefooted, she preferred just having bare legs. Even her teachers scolded her at school for pulling at her clothes and fidgeting in her seat.

In good weather, Anna enjoyed walking to school, but during stormy days and in the cold of winter, she did not want to leave the house at all.

The winter of 1929 was a record cold year even though there was little snow on the ground. She remembered the wood stoves in her house burning day and night. Many people in the area drank toasted barley coffee to keep warm, but Anna did not like the bitter taste, so her mother made tea or hot chocolate for her. Sometimes children from school would make excuses to come over just to have a cup of hot chocolate, because chocolate was rare and hard to find. Neighborhood children loved coming to Anna's house especially for holidays because Anna's family had special sweets shipped from Trieste, she could offer them.

Below is a letter Anna wrote which describes the unique customs of her family's Austrian Christmas celebrations.

Dear Allyson,

I want to tell you how our family celebrated Christmas. I grew up in a modest farming village where most everyone was poor. No one expected presents for Christmas. The war had left Friuli in great economic turmoil. When I was young, the Italians had not yet adopted the German Custom of a decorated tree with presents in their homes. Their only decoration was a nativity scene set up in the church in time for a special Christmas Mass.

I was lucky because my parents were Austrians, and we celebrated Christmas in a traditional German way. A few months before Christmas, I would go into the forest with some school friends to dig up moss so it would be dry by Christmas. My mother would place the moss on the table around pine branches that were bound with colored ribbon. She placed the branches into a large jar of water to crate our Christmas tree. The whole house had the fresh sent of pine. There were few pine trees in the area, except for the pines my mother and her first husband had planted near our house.

After my mother placed the moss around the tree, we would arrange cardboard figures of angels and little lambs around a nativity scene. The only present under t the tree was usually a box of chocolates from my aunts in Trieste, which we would share with family and friends.

Our tree was decorated with colored glass bulbs, a Father Christmas figurine, a chimneysweeper, and angels clipped onto the branches holding out their arms with candles to be lit at night. There were also small candies wrapped in bright colored paper, tied to the branches.

On a table, my mother placed a little candleholder with angels and a bell that would ring when the candleholder was lit. The heat would move a little fan, which caused the angels to circle around and strike the bell. How delighted I was to hear it ring. I thought it to be a mysterious miracle and wondered how the angels moved by themselves. The candleholder came from Vienna, and I wondered what a glorious fairy tale city Vienna must be.

When I was eleven, I remember an especially wonderful Christmas Eve. My mother let me invite three other girls to help decorate our tree. Their mothers came also to share in our festivities. We decorated the tree in the drawing room with glass bulbs, ribbons, moss, and figurines. We were talking constantly and giggling with excitement. Our mothers were sitting in the kitchen visiting at the table. The kitchen was the warmest part of the house and it smelled wonderful, like the apple strudel my mother had made earlier that afternoon.

When the tree was decorated and the candles were lit, there was magic in the air. We all sang, holding hands and walking around the decorated table with the Christmas tree. I remember my mother and I singing "Silent Night, "Stile Nacht" in German. Everyone was delighted to hear my mother's beautiful voice. Later we moved to the kitchen for warm strudel, hot chocolate and tea flavored with rum. My mother gave each girl a piece of chocolate.

When the church bell rang, near midnight, we gathered our winter clothing from a huge pile on the bed and happily walked, arm in arm, to the church in the center of Visco for Midnight Mass. As soon as we left the house, we were in a completely different world. The countryside was covered with snow and, even though the night was dark, the snow glistened and sparkled by the light of the moon. Most of the snow had blown across the road, revealing deep ruts from the farm wagons and carts. These ruts had filled with ice, and the moon glistened on them like shining strips of ribbon for us to follow and to skate on. I was convinced that the reason that snow was pure white was because the Christmas angels had sent it down to earth to make everything clean and white for baby Jesus to appear.

The Christmas Mass lasted for about an hour. When we came from the church, my mother and I said good night to our friends and walked home together. I studied the tracks in the snow that my friends and I had made on the way to Mass, and I wondered where our individual paths would take us.

Love, Anna Maria

***

Sometimes Anna would go into Visco to see if Maria Pasqualis could come out to play. At that time, Maria was twelve years old, three years older than Anna. Her mother, Leontina, was a widow, and Maria's father had been a coachman for a wealthy family but had died when Maria was young. Even though Leontina and Maria lived in a large old house in the center of Visco, the family was extremely poor and had little chance for income.

The two girls were very opposite in personalities but became friends out of a necessity for companionship. Maria was shy and quiet and would sit in the window seat hiding in the shadows but would occasionally peek out to watch activity in the town square. Sometimes Anna would go by Maria's house as late as twelve o'clock and Maria would still be in bed. Maria's mother encouraged her to stay in bed in the morning to save money on food by not serving breakfast. Leontina also gave Maria strict instructions to only walk on the road and not be seen running in public. Maria was never allowed to roam freely around the fields and farm paths, and as far as Leontina knew, she did not.

Leontina did not encourage visitors to come inside her house; oftentimes, she would even send Anna away. Sometimes in the afternoons, however, Maria and Anna were allowed to play with dolls and have pretend parties in the rear courtyard. They often looked through old magazines from Maria's older brother's collection where they found nice pictures and interesting articles about antiques, beautifully decorated palaces, history, and science.

Anna's mother, on the other hand, was accustomed to having afternoon tea and would often invite a friend with children to play with Anna. Mid-afternoon tea was not a custom in Italy, but ladies who came, enjoyed themselves immensely. Leontina would sometimes bring Maria when she visited Ida but did not encourage Anna or her mother to visit her own home.

Maria's own family seldom had company or guests. But Maria loved coming to Anna's house because she felt the freedom to laugh aloud and run freely. Maria was enchanted with how lively and talkative Anna and her family always seemed to be.

***

In the fall, Anna attended Visco Elementary School. She liked the social aspect of going to school but continued being only an average student. Because of her independent spirit, it was hard for her parents and teachers to discipline her. When Anna completed fifth grade, her parents decided to send her away to a private boarding school in Cividale. Ida's sisters encouraged and supported this decision because they felt Anna needed to learn discipline and self-control.

Cividale

The first time Anna took the entrances exam for Cividale, she did not pass, so her parents hired a tutor for the summer and the second time Anna took the exam she passed and was accepted into sixth grade.

In 1931, after summer vacation, her mother and Maria accompanied her to the convent where she would be staying for the school year. As they neared the convent, they arrived at a high bridge called Ponte Del Diavolo (Devil's Bridge). It was in the shadow of this bridge that Anna said goodbye to her mother and Maria and was taken by the nuns into the convent. Anna was twelve years old and away from her family for the first time.

The nuns suggested Ida should not come back for visits during the first year of school so Anna might learn self-control and curb her willful behavior through discipline and prayer. They also suggested that Anna not be allowed to return home until the end of the school year. Anna was surprised and deeply hurt that her mother would agree to these suggestions.

Anna hated the strictness of the nuns and their rigid rules. They scolded her often for daydreaming and not focusing on her schoolwork. She was miserable in these new surroundings. The other girls made fun of her and teased her for being so small. Anna had always been small for her age, but in the past, everyone thought she was cute. Now, Anna was made to feel inferior in both stature and intellect, and for the first time in her life, she lacked self-confidence and did not like herself.

Her imagination took her away on grand adventures in which she was able to "fly away" like Lindberg. It was hard for Anna to sit still and be quiet in the stale, stuffy classrooms, and through the long, boring periods of silence while the nuns prayed. She deeply missed her family, especially her mother, and the freedom she had growing up.

The convent had high arches and tall pillars surrounding a central courtyard. In the center of the courtyard was a large garden, in which the children played hide-and-seek and engaged in outdoor projects and activities. There was a tiny chapel at one end that was dark and cool, and Anna liked hiding there where, many times, no one found her. There were many bushes, pine trees, and flowers planted around a water fountain in the center of the courtyard. The only thing Anna enjoyed about being at the convent was playing outside in that garden.

Each day at six o'clock in the morning, the children woke up and prepared for Mass at seven o'clock. By 7:30, breakfast was served, and classes started at 8:30 a.m. lasting until 12 noon. The children were allowed to play for one hour each day. Some days, instead of playing, they would leave the convent and go on an excursion through the ancient city of Cividale.

For Christmas that year, all the girls were allowed to go home, except for Anna. She had to stay in the convent with the nuns and servants. For days, she cried and pouted, throwing tantrums because she wanted to go home. A servant cut some branches from a pine tree and brought them to Anna in a vase so she could have a Christmas tree. "This is not a Christmas tree!" she pouted. "I want a real Christmas tree with real decorations!" Anna cried angrily. "I don't understand why I can't go home or why my mother hasn't come to visit me!"

There were two elder nuns who were sweet and kind to Anna. When Mother Superior was not around, they brought her a small piece of cake, which Anna enjoyed and thanked them. Little by little, she began to conform to the strict rules and started to practice self-discipline and proper manners. Her tantrums became less frequent.

Finally, in late spring the next year, her mother arrived to take her home for summer vacation. Ida found her little girl was greatly changed and appreciated how mature and mannerly Anna had become.

Chapter 5
Middle School and Becoming a Young Lady

*B*efore World War II started, silk production was a major means of support for many people in Friuli. Anna's father ordered Silkworm eggs were ordered from Castel Franco by mail, and when they arrived in a small envelope, they were placed in a warm room for several days to hatch. When the tiny black worms were hatched, they were smaller than little black ants. These worms would go through four distinct cycles of eating and sleeping before they could begin their work of spinning silk.

For the first cycle, trays were prepared with mulberry tree leaves, cut into small thin pieces. When the worms were placed into the tray and would start sucking the juice from the leaves. Leaves had to be freshly cut every three hours, even throughout the night. Anna and her family took shifts cutting leaves. After one week of eating, the worms would sleep for a day or so, doubling their size. By the third cycle, they were about two and a half centimeters long. After that, they were able to suck the juice from whole leaves. The dry leaves had to be cleaned from the tray frequently and thrown out. After the fourth cycle, the worms were five centimeters long and were given entire branches of leaves to climb on and eat from.

The work intensified because piles of branches had to be cut to satisfy their growing appetites. After some eight to ten days, the worms were ready to be placed among the branches to start spinning their cocoons.

It was a messy business and trays had to be cleaned of excrements regularly.

Anna worked alongside her mother and father collecting branches and cleaning them. The worms would spin and weave for more than a week before their cocoons were woven. Once completed, the cocoons were gathered from branches and laid on large sheets to be cleaned and packed into large sacks and sold in Castel Franco.

The entire project took about eight weeks or so, but it was a strenuous and time-consuming project. For people of this region, profits from the sale of silk were more than enough to pay taxes and help buy farm supplies, or some cloth to make new clothing. Anna rejoiced when the season was over and everyone seemed to be in good spirits again.

During this time, Ida's only financial concern were the debts her eldest son, Dolfi, continued to accumulate. He was still living with her parents in Trieste but had grown up to be a lazy, selfish troublemaker. He often required money from Ida to cover his drinking and gambling debts. When she could, she satisfied Dolfi's debts by using her own pension, warning him to stop gambling and become more responsible. But rather than being grateful, Dolfi continued his reckless behavior until he was caught stealing money from his job at the Post Office, which Ida had arranged for him.

Unable to satisfy the huge post office debt, Ida was forced to appeal to Pepi for help, so Pepi reluctantly sold his beautiful riding horse to cover Dolfi's debts. Dolfi's supervisor had known Ida and her family for many years and, as a favor to her, did not press charges or report Dolfi to the police. From that point on, Dolfi became a constant source of irritation between Ida and her husband. Pepi resented the fact that Dolfi was taking advantage of her, and he was angry with Ida for allowing Dolfi's reckless behavior to continue without any real consequences.

Dolfi decided he would like to go to the United States and make a fresh start but would need enough money to make the trip and re-establish himself there. Ida and Pepi gave him a generous amount of start-up and travel money, but instead of leaving for the U. S., he went on a long trip around Europe by car with his friends until he ran out of money.

When he returned to Trieste, empty-handed, Ida appealed to the Post Office manager to rehire Dolfi. It was only a matter of time before he stole money a second time for which he was not forgiven. He was immediately arrested and sent to prison in Sardinia.

When his prison sentence was over, he returned to Trieste to live with his grandparents again but could not hold a job. He continued to blame others for all his misfortune. Eventually, he insisted that Ida and Pepi continue to support him, saying he deserved an income from the farm as part of his inheritance from his father.

Anna remembered Dolfi as being proud and arrogant. She would often accompany her mother to check on him in Trieste while also visiting other relatives and friends. She enjoyed staying with her aunts, even though they often criticized her for being too active and precocious. As she grew older, she found their household too restrictive and boring. She liked the excitement of being in the city but preferred the freedom she felt in the country.

Springtime was always Anna's favorite time of the year. In March, the early spring daisies and violets were blooming, and fields were turning green again. Anna excitedly wandered from one farm to the next to see which new animals were being born, and to watch little chicks and ducklings hatch.

***

Fedrico was still living at home and commuted by bike some thirty kilometers each day to Monfalcone. He worked as a designer and a draftsman for shipbuilders and airplane manufactures. He would bring home magazines with pictures of airplanes and stories about Lindberg and other pilots which excited Anna's imagination. She became engrossed with the new developments in air travel, continuing to dream of becoming a pilot.

Her other brother, Piero, had been taking agricultural classes, but was lazy and not a good student. When he came home for the summer, he went drinking with friends and refused to help Giuseppi (Pepi) on the farm. Usually he was quiet and harmless, but when he started drinking, Piero became reckless and irresponsible.

One winter evening, he went to town with their horse and buggy. Several boys were with him, and they kept the horse running all the way by using the whip. When they stopped at the bar, the poor, overheated horse was left outside in the cold for many hours. Though the horse made it home that night, it soon developed pneumonia and died. This incident proved to be the breaking point for Pepi's patience with Piero. Much to Ida's distress, he was no longer welcomed in their home. Piero grew to despise Pepi and resented the attention Ida gave him.

***

That fall, Anna returned to school in Cividale and had matured enough to understand the importance of obeying rules and exercising self-discipline. Her second year at Cividale went much better. That Christmas, her mother came to visit, bringing a box of sweets. Ida arrived early in the morning, and they sat together in the large visiting room till she left late that evening. Ida visited once more during Easter vacation.

***

During that year, Fedrico entered into the military, and after studying Morse Code, was assigned to Livorno as a Naval officer. In the summer, Anna and Ida anxiously anticipated his visits and when he came home, they greeted him with joy and excitement. He was an avid reader in several languages and had taught himself English. He brought new books and magazines on many subjects for the rest of the family to read. Each time he left for duty; he would leave them in his room for Anna to keep. She delighted in pouring over them again and again, igniting her imagination.

Fedrico had grown into a tall, good-looking man with a commanding presence, with clear blue eyes and dark hair which he combed straight back tight to his head. While he enjoyed playing sports and skiing, his passion was motorcycle riding.

After finishing his military obligations, he returned to Monfalcone and re-established himself at the shipyard, becoming head of his department. Usually he wore a nice camel-colored coat along with a black bowler hat. Even when he was casually dressed, he looked elegant, and Anna was proud to let people know he was her brother. He became involved in the local drama club and became a talented and celebrated actor.

***

Each summer, away from school, Anna enjoyed revisiting the farms around Visco and re-establishing her friendship with Maria who had not written while Anna was away at school. She later found out that Maria had difficulty with writing. Ida offered to loan Maria's mother, Leontina, money so Maria could go to private school with Anna, but Leontina did not want to be obligated to anyone, so Maria stayed at home.

Maria was always happy when Anna returned from school for the summer. She could laugh and act silly because Anna encouraged her to have fun. It was totally different than living under her mother's watchful eye, where her movements were precise and somewhat restricted. When she was with Anna, she became more animated and expressive.

***

Anna's last year at Cividale was her best year. Through determination, she excelled in all her classes and regained her sense of confidence. By the time she left, many of the nuns expressed true affection for her.

In the fall of 1935, Anna was enrolled in another private boarding school closer to home in Gorizia. She was excited about the new school because it was a large school less restrictive and in a more progressive city than the town of Cividale. Anna was already familiar with Gorizia because she had traveled there many times with her mother.

It was during her first year in Gorizia that Anna met her dearest friend, Nives, who was one year older and watched over Anna like a big sister, protecting her from snobby girls at school.

Nives, from a very wealthy family in Trieste, would invite Anna to visit her family on long weekends. She wore the latest fashions and had many colored dresses and pairs of shoes with matching handbags. Anna adored her style.

The school had International students from many backgrounds and Anna found their different languages and cultures fascinating. Anna like to entertain everyone by acting out scenes of plays and striking poses like those she saw on models from magazines.

One day, the director of the school saw Anna striking a sexy pose on the playground and scolded her in front of the other girls. Most of them laughed and made her feel ashamed. The director told Anna she looked ugly and vulgar, obviously referring to the playful pose. When Anna returned to her room, Nives was the only one who consoled her.

Anna wrote a letter to her mother asking for permission to leave the school, because she felt embarrassed. But Nives took Anna's letter to the director's office and said that if Anna left the school, she would report the director's rude behavior and would also leave the school. The director was forced to apologize to Anna. From then on, the director was less critical and more careful, especially in public.

***

During summer vacation that next year, Nives came to visit Anna in Visco for long periods of time. Anna also took frequent trips to Trieste with her mother to visit her aunts and to spend more time with Nives and her friends. They went to many nice villas for parties where they could dance and meet other young people.

One day, when Anna and her mother were on their way to the dressmaker in Santa Maria La Longa when they met a German-speaking girl named Wilma with her mother who also spoke German. Anna invited them back to their house where everyone spent a lovely afternoon speaking German together. This was the beginning of a friendship between Anna and Wilma that lasted many years.

***

In the early summer of 1936, there was great excitement in Anna's household because her favorite brother, Fedrico, was getting married. He and his new wife later established their home in Monfalcone, closer to Trieste, where he continued to be employed at the shipyards. He became president of the local motorcycle club and would often ride his motorcycle to Visco, visiting Anna and Ida on Sundays throughout that summer.

In October, Anna returned to school in Gorizia. She was now fourteen years old and enjoyed being around other intellectual and independent-minded young girls. She so enjoyed stimulating discussions and fierce debates. She had become a cultured, intelligent, and lovely young lady.

Chapter 6
Giorgio Becomes Anna's Tutor

*I*n the fall of 1936, Fedrico, was killed in a motorcycle accident at age twenty-six after only six months of marriage. Because his body was sent directly to his young wife in Monfalcone, Anna and her mother could not attend his funeral.

Anna mourned greatly over Fedrico's death, so Nives stayed close to her, helping cope with the tremendous loss she felt. Anna regretted being away from her mother during this period because Ida's letters to Anna also reflected deep suffering and profound sadness.

That following spring, when Anna returned to Visco, she noticed her mother had become withdrawn and was neglecting herself. Ida wore torn clothing and scuffed, dirty shoes. Even her hair was loose and unkempt. For the first time in her life, Anna was ashamed of the way her mother presented herself. No matter what Anna did, Ida could not shake her sadness over the loss of Fedrico.

Ida's other son, Piero, offered no comfort or support. By now, he was married with two children, but no longer visited or wrote letters home. Anna decided her mother needed companionship and insisted she would not return to school in Gorizia that fall. Ida agreed and arranged for a private tutor so Anna could continue with her German and French lessons.

The next three years were good for Anna. She continually met new friends from nearby villages and went to grand parties in nice villas. She continued practicing her German by writing letters to her aunts and other relatives in Trieste. But nothing made her happier than when Nives came to visit in the summer.

Behind Anna's house were many fruit trees, including several varieties of plums, grapes, and a few fig trees. Anna and her friends gathered fruit and had picnics under shade trees in the fields, dreaming of excitement and romance. Sometimes they went to the Italian Cavalry Post in Palmanova for some innocent flirting with soldiers stationed there.

Because Anna was so short, she looked younger than her actual age of sixteen; men did not take her seriously and treated her more like a little sister. This was even more pronounced when Anna played with her little puppy, Schnucki. Schnucki was a small, scruffy dog who provided lots of fun and entertainment wherever they went. Schnucki became her constant companion and a jealous guard dog when strangers would approach.

Since Anna was not enrolled in school now, Ida hired Giorgio, the son of a friend of hers in Cervignano, to tutor Anna in French and to further her education. Giorgio was six years older than Anna and a language student at Ca' Foscari University in Venice. Giorgio also studied math and history and spoke English, Italian, German, and French. He was an elegant man, tall, handsome, intelligent, and always well-dressed. Everyone seems to be drawn to him. He also played violin and was an accomplished artist. Anna didn't realize it at the time, but Giorgio would become one of the most important people in her life.

Giorgio
tutor and friend

Giorgio on his way to Capri
1951

Giorgio lived with his mother and aunt near the central square of Cervignano. They had a beautiful villa once owned by Napoleon Bonaparte's sister and family with a large private garden in the back of the house hidden from the street.

Giorgio's mother had been a professional cook for an ambassador in Trieste and baked wonderful cakes and breads. She always prepared meals in an artistic way and her presentations were magnificent, especially for holidays. Holidays were made extra special by her delicious, beautiful meals and elaborate parties. Conversations at these gatherings were inspiring and informative because the participants were intelligent and cultured. Anna immensely enjoyed being at these events with Giorgio and in this way was introduced into the local aristocratic Italian society.

She rode her bicycle fifteen kilometers to Giorgio's for lessons two or three times a week and sometimes, after a long lesson with him, Giorgio's mother would invite Anna to spend the night. Anna developed a deep affection for him and his family.

In 1939, Benito Mussolini joined Italy into the Axis Alliance with Germany and Japan against the other European countries. Later that year, Giorgio was called to join the Italian army as an officer. He left for Rome at the beginning of WWII. While away, he wrote Anna beautiful letters in several languages, often including jokes and riddles, which she would solve and send back to him. In this way, he continued to tutor her. She cherished every one of his letters and read them many times. He told about his training and the kinds of people he met. He described people so vividly and in such great detail like an artist would have painted them.

Then, on a parachute landing near Rome, he fell and broke his leg. Soon after, he was discharged and sent home to recuperate. He and Anna resumed their lessons three times a week. At this point, he did not charge her mother for lessons because he liked practicing languages with her and also because he no longer thought of her a pupil, but as a dear friend.

In the fall of that year, Giorgio returned to school in Venice to complete a degree in English at Ca' Foscari Language University. He was away from Cervignano for long periods of time but continued to write Anna. He told her about the beautiful Venetian palaces he had visited and the parties he attended.

Anna adored and admired Giorgio but knew he had many friends and companions at the university that demanded his attention. She began spending more time socializing with the other young people in Palmanova.

In 1941, the Italian cavalry had a large base in Palmanova and there was much military activity in the area with soldiers coming and going, often on horseback. During this time, Anna met an Italian officer named Domenico at a café in Palmanova who was ten years her senior. She found him polite and intelligent. He was tall and handsome with blue eyes and brown hair.

They started seeing each other on a regular basis and after a few dates, he informed her that he had received orders to go to Africa and would be leaving soon.

Their relationship intensified, and after many attempts on his part, they finally made love. Anna preferred keeping the relationship light and fun, but he constantly wanted to dominate her and monopolize her time demanding a more intimate relationship. She thought that he would soon be gone, and their relationship would end, but around the time he was due to leave, his shipping orders were canceled. They continued to see each other but he became increasingly more possessive and jealous, so they often quarreled. One day, Domenico told Anna that studying other languages was a waste of time for a woman, and that Anna should learn more useful skills that would aid her in becoming a good wife. She tried to distance herself from him and stopped going to Palmanova as often as she had been going. When Domenico could not find Anna in town, he started to come to her house in Visco looking for her.

Anna began hiding from him and trying to avoid being alone with him because he was always pulling at her and begging to make love. When she turned him down, he accused her of having other lovers, and tried to make her feel ashamed and childish for not letting him have his way. Finally, his orders came, and he was shipped out to Africa.

Anna was overjoyed when he left. He wrote letters and tried to make plans for when he would return, but Anna was tired of him and began dreading the day he would come back. She seldom answered his letters. Then, later that year, one of his friends told her that Domenico had been killed in Africa. She also learned he had been married to a woman in southern Italy for many years, and they had a child together. She felt angry and humiliated and did not feel any deep remorse for his death.

***

It was now summer of 1942. Giorgio was home from the university and their regular lessons in English resumed. Her lessons at Giorgio's home were more like long, leisurely visits. His aunt served them tea with lemon and cakes and other nice sweets. They had a nice private room in which to study, but some afternoons, Anna and Giorgio went for long walks while they practiced speaking in several languages. They played word games and sometimes made up poetry. Then, late afternoons would stop at a café for a drink before Anna rode her bike home.

***

Giorgio and his friends often had small parties in Cervignano and in the surrounding villages where his friends lived. Anna was invited because she was entertaining and loved to dance. Giorgio encouraged her to make up skits they would act out together entertaining all the others. When these parties lasted late into the evening, Giorgio's mother insisted Anna stay the night.

These modest parties and gatherings took people's minds off the dire economic situation during the war in Italy. All of Europe was experiencing a food shortage and most everything was already being rationed. But Anna, Giorgio, and their friends continued to enjoy the company of each other.

Chapter 7
Under German Occupation

*B**y** 1943, the German invasion* was in full swing throughout Italy. There was no train service at this time in northern Italy, and no law enforcement officials other than soldiers in military uniform. The Germans took over the military barracks and the town of Palmanova when the Italian cavalry was shipped out. Germans controlled all traffic in the area and the invasion established new fears throughout northeastern Italy. Even though the Italian and German armies were allied, the Italian Partisans were continuously fighting the Germans and causing unrest in the villages.

Many people were tortured for information by both sides: the German army and later by Italian Partisans.

Non-commissioned German soldiers stayed in the barracks at Palmanova, however, the officers established themselves in the homes of local villagers. Anyone with an extra bedroom was obligated to house German officers. A military doctor, his wife and three children were the first Germans to stay in Anna's home. They were happy that Anna and her family spoke German and were kind and considerate throughout their stay.

After the German family left, only high-ranking German officers stayed with Anna's family. Her family had to give up their parlor for the officers to use as a meeting room. The German officers also occupied two bedrooms upstairs. Some officers were nice and greeted Anna's family upon meeting them; others were stern and did not want to be bothered by any interaction.

Anna, her father, and mother, and brother, Guido sat at the small kitchen table during mealtimes and in the evenings, keeping as quiet as possible. Never asking questions, they kept to themselves and minded their own business. Ida and Anna were respectful, polite, and kept the house clean.

As time went by, the Germans began to interact more with the family. They sometimes had extra food and would offer it to the family as a way of saying thanks. The only traumatic event was when "Schnucki" was crushed in the road by a fast-moving military vehicle. Anna and her father buried him in a field where they used to play.

One day when Anna was visiting her friend, Wilma, she saw that many wounded soldiers were hospitalized in the villa next to Wilma's home. As they stood in front of Wilma's house, a military car passed by with Wilma's friend, Karl, driving. Beside him sat a German major. They stopped to visit for a few minutes, and Anna was impressed with how eloquently the major spoke. When they left, Anna told Wilma she would like to see the major again.

The next time Wilma had a chance to talk with Karl, she told him about Anna's sentiment. That following weekend, Karl, and the major invited Wilma and Anna to a party in Cervignano. Wilma rode her bike to Anna's house so they could be picked up together. It was November, and already dark, when Karl and the major arrived that evening in a large black German car to pick up the two girls. The major had several escorts equipped with guns and there was great commotion when they entered the house. Everyone was speaking German, and the soldiers felt comfortable and at home in this German household. Anna's mother brought out cakes and her father brought out wine.

Later, they played music on the record player and people began dancing. Wilma became angry when they never ended up going to the party and left early to bike home alone.

During the evening, the major asked for permission to stay the night because they had been drinking and everyone was tired. Anna gave the major her room, and the others slept on the floor in the sitting room.

Later that night, Anna went to see if the major was comfortable (and maybe give him a few kisses) but when she entered the room, he was already snoring and sound asleep. She quietly left and slept in her brother's room. The following morning, when Anna woke up at eight, the men had already gone. Anna regretted not being able to say goodbye.

Another time, Wilma invited Anna to a Christmas party in Palmanova to meet several other girls with whom she had gone to school. Anna was happy just to be with Wilma and spend time away from home even though she didn't know any of the other girls, she found them to be boring and uninteresting. They all made polite conversation though and noticed two German naval soldiers had entered the room. One was an officer, the other an enlisted man. Anna had not met anyone from the Navy before and wondered what they were doing in Palmanova so far from the seaport. It surprised her when the tall, slender officer came over and asked her to dance. Anna felt a bit shy because he was so tall and handsome, and she felt like a little mouse (*topolino*) next to him. He laughed with delight when he learned that Anna spoke perfect German and introduced himself as Herman Fecker.

Around five-thirty that evening, as it began to get dark, Anna announced that she had to return home. Herman offered to accompany her by bike part of the way, or at least as far as the villa where he was staying. When they arrived at his villa, he invited her in. She was curious to see where he lived but was also a little afraid that he might try something inappropriate. However, she liked him enough to feel she could trust him to be a gentleman, therefore, agreed to go in. He led her into a large room set up like a parlor. He played Christmas records and as she walked around the room singing softly, he ordered tea, biscuits, and chocolates from the kitchen staff. Anna was impressed because she had not had tea or tasted chocolate for over a year. Because he remained respectful and polite Anna had a wonderful time.

When the clock finally struck seven, Anna said she had to bike straight home because her family would be worried and waiting up for her. Herman insisted on accompanying her all the way home saying it was too dangerous for a young girl to be riding around in the countryside alone at night. Anna was delighted and as they walked, she thought how regal he looked in his naval uniform, a dark blue double-breasted coat with golden buttons and rank insignias on his sleeves. He walked straight and proud as he pushed her bicycle alongside of him. Anna found it hard to believe that such a wonderful looking man was interested in her company.

It was cold and the wind whipped at their faces. The sky was dark and clear, and they could hear church bells ringing from the nearby villages. Anna was reminded of a Christmas Eve one read about in fairy tales, complete with the handsome prince walking next to her.

By the time they reached home, it was nearly eight o'clock. Anna's mother was the only one still awake and waiting up for her. The fire was out in the kitchen, but Ida stoked it up to make pancakes and ham for them. After the meal and some small talk, Herman left. Ida told Anna she was astonished to see such a handsome young man in her home and agreed that he looked just like a prince. That night, Anna and her mother talked about romance and laughed a long time before going to bed.

The next day, Wilma came by to ask if they could meet at Anna's house the following week. The following Sunday afternoon, Herman and another naval soldier, Heinz, arrived with a record player and dance records. Wilma was jealous that Herman seemed more interested in Anna and that she was stuck with the less elegant, enlisted man. Being a mischievous type, Wilma was tempted to cut the ribbons hanging from Heinz's cap. But Anna discouraged her because it would have been terribly disrespectful.

It was a sunny day, but cold, even for January. They all stayed in the drawing room, warmed by the fire and the wood stove. Then they danced and talked about languages and customs of countries around the world. Everyone enjoyed the day so much they planned another encounter at Anna's house the following week.

As February approached, it became the time of year when all of Italy was celebrating "Carnivale" with parties, costumes, processions, and special foods. Carnivale celebrations ended on Shrove Tuesday, the day before the beginning of Lent. Ida filled a platter with several kinds of traditional sweets, which were all made with a similar type of fried dough, garnished with raisins, cinnamon, nutmeg, and cardamom. Another traditional type of treat was *crostoli*, long thin strips of dough, fried until they were crispy and dipped into a tureen of freshly whipped cream.

Later that evening, Anna and her mother sat together satisfied and happy to have spent such a lovely day in the company of the nice young men. That following week, Anna took her horse and rig to Palmanova where they all met at a *ristorante* for a nice meal and a game of *bocce* ball. When the evening was over, they said good-bye to the two Navy men at Palmanova Centro. On the way back home, Anna passed by Wilma's house to drop her off, then took the long way home on the small dirt farm roads dreaming of the past weeks of lovely memories.

The war seemed far away, and the countryside was peaceful, except for the sound of a plane from time to time. Even with a war going on, these days were happy and carefree. Anna was grateful for so much free time since most young girls her age had to work on farms or do housework inside of homes. Ida, however, had a good housemaid, was who liked Anna and encouraged her to go out and have fun while she was still young. Anna was twenty-one years old, and in the prime of her life. She was optimistic about being married one day and having children.

The following Sunday, Herman, Heinz, and Wilma came back to Anna's. Ida cooked a strudel piled with apples, raisins and sugar, and everyone sang German songs. The men said that being at Anna's made them feel they were at home in Germany.

When Anna and Herman were alone on the sofa, he looked at her silently, then reached over and kissed her. Anna moved closer to him, and when he shifted his body, he sat on a pillow in such a way that it split open. Feathers flew into the air, some sticking to his uniform and some swirling to the floor. They burst out laughing and giggling while trying to collect the loose, flying feathers. Since Herman was usually quiet and dignified, the situation seemed even funnier to Anna. Everyone came into the room to see what the commotion was about. After spending another wonderful day together, Herman and Heinz accompanied Wilma home.

Within days, the girls learned the men had been suddenly shipped out to Greece without having time to say good-bye. Anna wondered if their ship had left from Venice or Trieste. She also wondered what was going through their minds as they left the peaceful Italian countryside for the dangers of war.

About a month later, Wilma came to Anna's house by bike. Her eyes were red and face puffy. Anna immediately knew something was wrong.

"I just talked to some navel soldiers in Palmanova," she said. "and the ship Herman and Heinz were on was blown up, with few survivors!" The girls cried together, trying to console each other.

After Wilma left, Anna went for a long walk and cried as hard as she could. That incident ended her brief encounter with the German Navy. Soon the Navy unit left, and the *Luftwaffe,* a German Air Force unit. moved into the area. All things in the area were about to change again.

From Anna: The German Air Force (Luftwaffe)

These air force units started moving into the area in small groups. There were never many soldiers in any one group, I suppose because the Germans had their troops fighting throughout Europe. Several units were staying nearby at St. Maria La Longa, near Udine, in the Count Melzi Villa. My friend, Wilma, was usually familiar with troop movements throughout the area because her father was a German engineer and sometimes socialized with German officers. One day, she came to my house by bike and excitedly announced that a highly decorated group of Air Force officers had arrived and were staying near her house. I was excited and enthusiastic about meeting people from the Luftwaffe because I always dreamed of becoming a pilot. Just by associating with these pilots, I felt the possibility of one day being able to fly myself. Wilma and I went immediately to the office they had opened at the villa to make ourselves known. There were several airmen and one captain working in the office. We welcomed them in German. They seemed quite happy to have been received in Italy by two German-speaking country girls. We started a little conversation and explained our German connections. I told them that I came from another village, seven kilometers away, and that my parents were Austrians.

There were two warrant officers staying at Wilma's house. Wilma was rather taken by one of these men, even though she knew that he was already married. He was a chemist from Hamburg, genuinely nice, and Wilma continued to flirt with him. After he had been living in their home for a while, he received a telegram from German that his son was born. Wilma, being of a jealous nature, grabbed his gun and began to shoot wildly around the yard. What a commotion she created! Everyone was scared, until the gun was emptied.

It was the spring of 1944 when the Luftwaffe unit arrived in our area. All of nature spoke of springtime. It was easy for everyone to forget the war. The warm sunshine put everyone in high spirits for the festivities of Easter. On Good Friday, a few officers appeared at my house to surprise me with a bird's nest. In the nest there were a few chocolate eggs. In the center of the nest was a small shield with a heart, which signified their unit. I had never expected such a friendly gesture from these soldiers, and it overwhelmed me with emotion. We had not tasted chocolate for years. I felt proud to be included in their familiar circle.

They had come to invite me to participate in a supper at the commander's villa for Easter Monday. This was a medical detachment that was stationed at the main villa in Tissano. The colonel in command had a little airplane, by which he could take off and land from the villa's large garden.

On Monday, a shiny black car came to get me, in which there were three officers, one more handsome than the next. One of the officers was from Berlin and was without one arm. He had been a parachutist and told us that an American pilot had shot him while he was underneath his parachute. I felt deeply sorry for him. He said he would soon be dismissed and would be going back home.

It was six o'clock in the evening when we arrived in Tissano. As we entered the dining room of the villa, there was a nice big oval table already laid out for supper. There were 17 officers standing around the table, and then I was seated next to the commander. As I looked around, I was astonished to be the only girl. We started with small talk about the area and with much humor, I told them stories of the customs and the people of that area. The name of my village is Visco, and I explained this word meant "Voge Ieim," a glue to catch birds with. I made them all laugh I expressed myself in German.

After a while, they put some nice music on the Victrola, and the one-armed officer asked me to dance. We danced into the main entrance hall, which was lit with the last rays of the sunset. The long beams came through the branches of the large trees around the garden. This officer danced very well and had a syncopated step, which was still not practiced in much of Europe. I was a born dancer and could easily follow him. We all enjoyed the evening very much. At one point I told the commander that I wished to join my friend Wilma, who was going to attend another party at Villa Melzi. He ordered some officers to escort me to the second party. I had two escorts, plus the driver; one soldier sat in front with the driver and two were in the back with me. I felt like a princess being delivered to a ball.

The dance had already started at the Villa Melzi when we arrived. There were more women than men in the crowd, and the three officers who had escorted us decided to stay. The atmosphere was warm and nice, so we easily mixed into the crowd. There was a record player playing dance music, and an accordion player who circled around playing an occasional tune. I kept dancing with the one-armed officer. We decided to go outside in the garden to cool off. It was there that he told me that he was leaving for Berlin the next day. We kissed each other and it was like a dream. When we returned to the party, we continued to dance until he became tired and sat down. I continued to dance with others to sort of show off for him. It was well after midnight when I decided it was time to go home. I felt sad when it was time to say good-bye, especially to this young officer. I could not have asked for a better escort, and it was a pleasure to have known him. This had been a very pleasant Easter, indeed!

Wilma asked the captain, she had been dancing with that evening, if he would take us by car to a place near Udine the next Sunday for a christening. It was too far to bike, and there was no organized public transportation at that time. He promised her that he would take us both the following Sunday.

When Sunday came, I went to Wilma's house, and we waited for the captain to pick us up. After waiting several hours, we started walking around to ask other soldiers where he was. No one seemed to know, so we decided to go back to the large villa to ask the commander if he knew where the captain could be. All was quiet at the villa, and no one seemed to be around. We found a little donkey running loose in the garden and, because I knew how to ride, I mounted the donkey and, as a joke, rode it into the entrance hall. This was the hall we had been dancing in the previous week. At this point, all the men came out of the large ballroom where they had been conducting a meeting. Even though they smiled at me, they seemed somewhat serious. The captain was indeed there, and he explained that he had several important briefings to attend before he could pick us up at Wilma's.

Later that evening, we found out why everyone was acting so serious. All of the soldiers had been ordered to move farther south to the battlefront in the mountains between Florence and Bologna. One airman who had been ordered to the front had already killed himself. This was solemn news and sad to reflect on. We never saw these soldiers after that day. It was said that nearly all of them had been killed in the mountains near Monte Cassino.

Anna Maria Venturini

Chapter 8
The Partisans Become More Active

*B*y 1944, there was only a small concentration of soldiers stationed in Northern Italy at Palmanova. Thus, the Italian and
Yugoslav Partisans became more active in the area. These Partisans had been creating mischief in the area for the Germans
throughout the war, but now there were fewer soldiers to maintain
law and order.

The Italian Partisans, known as German Resistance Fighters,
wore green armbands and called themselves, "The Italian Soldiers
for Freedom." The Slavic Partisans were trained by Tito and wore
red armbands. Tito sent the Slavic Partisans into Italy to gain a
foothold and reclaim this region for Yugoslavia. The only thing
these two partisan groups had in common was a hatred for anyone
or anything German. They destroyed property throughout the area
and tortured people who spoke German. They had no legal authority but made their own laws, imposing themselves upon the
villages and farmers to feed and clothe them. The local people
were afraid of these rough and ill-mannered partisans.

Young women were especially fearful of these groups because girls were often taken away to be questioned, never to return home again. Villagers were reluctant to talk or complain about injustices they experienced and even became suspicious of each other. There were partisan spies everywhere and many stories circulated about partisan tactics of torture.

Food shortages also helped to make people more aggressive towards each other. It became common for neighbors to report one another for having extra meat, food, and rationed items. They also reported neighbors for having anything of value which the partisans would take.

At Anna's dressmaker's house, a visiting fascist smelled coffee and reported her. Later, her house was broken into, and many items were stolen. People's hearts had been hardened by the poverty and economic depression.

Anna's family, and a few others who had been obligated to house German officers, became targets for the partisans. One evening a group of partisans followed Anna home after she had been to a neighbor's house for supper. Her friend's family had a large house and had also housed German officers. The partisans wanted to question Anna about the officers who had stayed at her home and at her friend's house. They were suspicious because Anna's family spoke German and had many German items in their home. Indeed, Anna's mother had designed the house with trims typical of those found in Germany, and their house was not a typical Italian farmhouse.

That evening after following Anna home, the partisans banged on the door and before Anna could answer, pushed themselves inside, slamming the door behind them. Anna's parents came into the entrance hall to meet them when one shabby-looking, loud-mouthed man pointed to the parlor and told Ida and Pepi to take a seat and be quiet. He pulled on Anna's arm to lead her out of the room. The last thing Anna saw before she left was her mother nervously wringing her handkerchief and weeping softly. Her father stared straight past her without blinking.

Leading Anna into the kitchen, the partisans demanded she give them food. She brought out bread, cheese, and a pitcher of wine. While they ate, they asked her questions about her family and their connections to Germany. Her answers were short and to the point. The men also went through the cupboards, examining everything looking for food, money, or anything of value.

After grabbing more food, they found the door leading out of the kitchen to the storage room attached to the stables. Pushing Anna out the door ahead of themselves, they entered into the large storage area where her father stored old tools, wood, farm machinery, and supplies. This area was not well lit, and the floor uneven and made of cobblestone. Anna walked slowly and quietly so she would not lose her footing.

After examining the contents of the room, they wanted to inspect the animal stalls. Anna wondered if they were looking for her brothers or for anyone else whom they could intimidate.

As they mumbled amongst themselves, two of them stepped forward calling Anna a traitor to Italy.

"We're going to shave your head, so everyone will know you've been warned!" one of them yelled. When they stepped toward her, she grabbed a rake and stepped backward, holding it across her chest, threatening them with her posture and facial expression.

"You will not touch me!" she shouted at them. "I am Italian like you!" She told them her family had used their knowledge of German as a means of survival. "I know the Commander in Palmanova," she said when she saw them hesitate. "If you harm me, the Commander will hunt you down for harming innocent Italian citizens!" To prove her family had strong ties to the Italian military, she lied about them being stationed nearby. The men all laughed.

"This annoying little dog needs to be shut up, but it's not worth our time," they shouted. "Let's send this pup back to her parents." Finally, they dismissed her by throwing straw at her, and threatening to watch her house. Because she was so small in stature, she wondered if they thought of her as still being a child which may have saved her from being hurt worse.

Anna walked calmly back into the house and waited in the parlor with her parents until the partisans left. Ida and Pepi were left unharmed themselves but could see by Anna's messy hair and dirty clothing that she had been pushed around, but otherwise seemed all right.

Not long after that incident, they received news that Monte Cassino had fallen in the south to the Allies, and they suspected the war would soon be over as the Allied forces swept northward through Italy. It had taken seven months for the Allies to take the twenty kilometers of steep hills around Monte Cassino and was the hardest fought and deadliest battle in the Allied Campaign to take Italy. There were still scattered German patrols throughout northeastern Italy, but the Allies were slowly pushing them north and out into Austria.

"Anna, it is no longer safe for you to be here," her parents told her. "We want you to leave home for a while and to stay away until order is restored to the region."

The following evening, Anna packed some food and clothing and, under the cover of darkness, left home. She snuck out the back door, pushing her bike through the gate of the orchard fence, taking cover in the tall grass of the hayfield behind her house. She traveled near fence lines where overgrown bushes and trees helped to conceal her and continued on foot pushing her bicycle as she cut through the countryside. She stayed away from farmhouses and roads, afraid a dog might start barking and alert someone to her presence. Sometimes farmers shot into the darkness to scare intruders or thieves away.

As she worked her way southeast to Cervignano, more than fifteen kilometers away, she planned to go to where Giorgio's family lived. It was at least two o'clock in the morning when she left herself into their backyard gate. Since they were not expecting her, she did not want to disturb them in the middle of the night. So, she curled up on a wicker sofa on their back porch and waited until dawn.

The next morning, she told Giorgio, his mother and aunt about the incident at her house.

"You will come to Venice with me," Giorgio told her where he was completing his degree at Ca' Foscari. "I have many friends and contacts there and you will be in a safe place to wait out the last days of the war." Venice, an island city, was not situated near battlefields, or involved with troop movements.

The most difficult problem was how to travel to Venice. The trains had been shut down for years and with no public transportation, the only way to go to Venice was by foot or bike. The roads were still unpaved, and spring rains made them hard to travel on.

Anna and Giorgio set out on the two hundred-fifty-kilometer journey with a couple of rickety old bikes. Her tires were constantly going flat, and they had to make many stops to pump air into her tires. The trip took much longer than they intended as they followed the coastal footpaths along the rocky Adriatic shoreline.

Despite these setbacks, Anna still considered it a wonderful adventure, because she was happy to be alone with Giorgio. They talked about philosophy and astronomy, practiced different languages, and made-up words that rhymed, often combining two or more languages just for fun.

Once, while resting near the ancient Venetian town of Por-toguaro, they heard a heavily loaded allied plane approaching. Suddenly, it unloaded its bombs, destroying a train track on the outskirts of town. It was terrifying to hear the blast and see the black smoke rise. Throughout that day, they counted five more planes flying southward toward the Allied front which was now near Bologna. Each time they saw a plane, they stopped to watch, wondering where the bombs would be unloaded next. Later that day, they traveled past a fabric manufacturing plant that had been bombed the day before.

Finally, they arrived in Venice late that evening; their faces and arms were badly sunburned. The wind had also flattened and straightened their hair. Walking across many little footbridges, they arrived in the area of Venice called Dorsoduro, near Ca' Fos-cari, and presented themselves at the pensione, where Giorgio stayed when he was in Venice. Their clothes were filthy, and they were exhausted.

The lady who owned the pensione was happy to see Giorgio and welcomed Anna, who pulled out some polenta and a few hardboiled eggs she had saved from their journey.

"These are for you, signora," she said offering them to the lady.

Thank you so much, Anna, what a wonderful gift." People in the cities had suffered more from hunger than the farmers in the country. "Come in and rest."

Over the next weeks, everyone in the city was eager for news about the war on the mainland and crowded around radios to lis-ten for updates on the progress of the fighting. Venice functioned with a sort of uneasy peace. Finally, when Allied forces began taking control in northern Italy, Anna and Giorgio decided it was time to return home

Memory Album

Anna at 23 years of age

Anna at age 16 on a ferry boat

On a bike excursion

In a wheat field at her farm in Visco

Anna on her father's riding horse Visco

Anna's bus pass

Office staff at the Geological Institute Trieste

*Anna at her desk at Allied Headquarters
Udine*

*Anna in the doorway of her
childhood home
Visco 1966*

*Last photo taken with Pepi,
her father
1958*

Anna and Hilda in Venice
1968

Anna and Allyson at a local café
Aviano 1972

FROM: DMSCSC   15 July 1971

SUBJECT: Nomination for Outstanding Administrative Specialist

TO: DA

1. Miss Anna M. Venturini is nominated as the outstanding Administrative Specialist from the Supplies Management Branch of the 40th Supply Squadron. Miss Venturini has distinguished herself as being a highly knowledgeable person in administration procedures and how they relate to the supply system. She is called upon to quality control letters and messages which contain technical data that requires a general knowledge of supply procedures. Having an excellent memory she is able to remember supply facts that pertain to her job, and to recall them in a short period of time. In addition to this she is a person who is continuously discovering means to perfect her already outstanding methods of filing, typing and maintenance of publications. She has streamlined her job to enable her to do, for the last six months, a job that is authorized 3 people.

2. Miss Venturini is an energetic individual who is unselfish in her devotion to duty. Many times when emergency situations arise she volunteers to spend extra hours without pay to do the needed work. She is sensitive to the needs of her fellow 40th Supply Administrative personnel. When she discovers a problem area she volunteers to help solve the problem as well as provide suggestions for extra management action that are needed to prevent the problem from reoccurring. While doing this she uses diplomacy and tact in her contacts. Also in order to try and improve the framework of the system from within, she has become a contributor to the base suggestion program.

3. Miss Venturini has a cheerful attitude in her job performance. This boosts the morale of all who come in contact with her. She displays warmth for the people she meets and enthusiasm for the outstanding job she performs on a daily basis.

Sandra C. Nixon
SANDRA C. NIXON, 1Lt, USAF
OIC, Stock Control Section

Letter of her character

Department of the Air Force
40TH TACTICAL GROUP (USAFE)

SPECIAL

ACHIEVEMENT

AWARD

MISS ANNA M. VENTURINI

For Special Achievement Accomplished

SUSTAINED SUPERIOR PERFORMANCE AWARD

LOWELL D. COVINGTON, Colonel, USAF
Base Commander

10 December 1975

AF FORM 341, JUN 89   ☆ GPO : 1985 O—353-844

Certificate of Special Achievement

*Base commander presenting Anna the
Certificate of Achievement for her work*

Certificate of Achievement

*Maria (Pasqualis) Tei, Hilda, Anna
Mafalda, and Nevis Tei
in Perugia for Allyson's graduation ceremony*

*Anna at Sella Nevea
near Tarviso
A popular ski resort*

*Anna's 80th birthday with Allyson
attending an art workshop
Sorèze, France*

*Anna on a foot path above Trieste
2000*

**Elda Livot Simeon, Mafalda, and Allyson
visiting Anna's grave in Visco
near Elda's home
2008**

**Marina Gilletti waving from the
balcony of the house
Anna's grandparents built in Trieste
Currently owned by the Gilletti family**

Chapter 9
After the War

*A*s *Anna looked back at the war years,* there was one incident
that had made her more fearful than all the rest. She shared
that memory in a letter to me.

Dear Allyson,

*In March of 1945, until the end of April, a Cossack cav-
alry unit came to Visco with their commander, General Volkov.
They stayed at my house for two weeks. The war was ending, and
they were on the run, trying to escape the Allies. These Cossack
units of about 100 were mostly from the Ukraine and used by the
Germans to fight the Partisans who stayed concealed in the
mountains most of the time. But sometimes, the Partisans came
down to the villages in our area around Udine to procure food
and other things they needed. If any Partisans were caught, the
Cossacks killed them immediately. Sometimes the Partisans also*

ambushed the Cossacks. These skirmishes between them were fierce. Once, when a skirmish had ended, the Cossacks burned the whole village down because they suspected Partisans were hiding among the villagers. The people in Visco had heard stories about how fierce and brutal these Cossacks could be, so when they arrived in Visco, we were all desperately frightened of them. The population was very scared of these unusual and strange-looking Cossack soldiers. They were dirty, unkempt, and not groomed unlike any of the German soldiers we had seen with tailored uniforms and polished brass and boots. Their ill-fitted clothing was dark or gray in color, and their boots were worn and dusty. They treated all Italians with suspicion as they sought out Partisans. They used fierce looks and intimidating force to do what they wanted. They were excellent riders, and their horses were well-trained.

My prized and most useful possession was a bicycle. When a Cossack soldier stole it and rode it to town, I followed him and stole it back. Just as I was returning near my house, I heard a loud commotion behind me. I glanced back to see this soldier yelling at me. I quickly hid my bike in a field behind our barn and came into the house through the back door. I saw the Cossack on horseback coming right into the house through the open front door, yelling at me. I turned and ran up the stairs to the second floor. The horse's hoofs stomped on the wooden staircase making loud, terrifying noises as he followed me. I left the second floor and ran up the more narrow wooden spiral staircase to the attic. The horse panicked on the small staircase and became wedged in the turn. The Cossack had to back down the staircase, yelling the entire way. I was thinking that if he had come up after me, I would have had to climb out the window and onto the roof. I feared that if he caught me he would have killed me with his long sword. I waited silently, listening for a long time before returning down-stairs.

That year, the Cossacks decided to celebrate their Ortho-dox Easter in my house. They came to my father asking for wine and a goblet to use for their communion. My father had hidden a five-liter bottle of white wine for our own Easter celebration and did not want to give it up. One soldier had a gun in his hand and shook it at my father. My father just stood there saying nothing. At that time, I was unaware of what was going on in the kitchen and had already gone through a different door to the cellar to bring back a liter of wine I had also hidden. My father gave me a smile as if to say, "thank you." They all finished drinking our wine and, with loud laughter, prepared for the night. When we awoke in the morning, they were already gone.

Soon, the Allied forces arrived in great numbers, and for an entire month, we saw large convoys of soldiers moving west-ward, accompanied by military trucks, tanks, and motorbikes. These troops were well-equipped, especially the Americans, who had quantities of equipment unimaginable. The Americans brought with them canned hams, coffee, and chocolate, which they handed out to villagers along the way. We were so grateful, and this was the first time I realized how generous the American people were.

Many liberation troops flooded the area, dressed in dif-ferent uniforms. They came from England, Australia, New Zea-land, India, and, of course, the United States of America. There was little peace and no quiet in the countryside, especially the last few months before the war ended.

Northeastern Italy was a political and economic mess. The last battle of World War II was fought near Trieste. After forty days of fighting, the Allied forces declared a victory and re-turned Trieste to Italy. Allied Headquarters was established at

Castello Miramare in Trieste by the British and the American governments. They stayed in Trieste for ten years after the war ended to provide stability for the entire region.

Anna Maria Venturini

Several camps were set up around Visco to provide shelter for many people who had been displaced during the war. These camps operated for over two years after the war had ended because the people who lived there had nowhere to go and no means to move. Anna's mother would make food for them and share dried figs, lard for cooking, and baked goods once a week, which Anna would help her mother deliver to the camps.

In October 1945, Anna decided to go to Klagenfurt, Austria, with her friend, Wilma. During the last years of the war, Wilma had been sent to Klagenfurt by her grandparents because they feared the Partisans in our area. Being familiar with Klagenfurt, Wilma knew of employment opportunities and encouraged Anna to apply for work. They rode in a British military truck through the northern mountain passes near Sella Neva and Tarvisio. The truck ride was rough, even though they rode in the cab upfront and were grateful for the escort.

Anna and Wilma found employment as clerks for an auto manufacturer, ordering and requisitioning car parts. The following May, Anna decided to leave Austria to go home. The Italian government had set up roadblocks, and quarantine camps to hold and inspect all people before they were allowed to enter Italy. In some cases, people were held there at the border for over a month. Anna decided not to go through the border-controlled route into Italy and, instead, hired a guide in Villach to take her across the border with another small group of people. There were several Romanian citizens in this group, but most people were Italian, and simply wanted to return home.

The group started out early in the morning and walked all day until twelve midnight when they arrived at a little chalet, especially prepared for groups of people making their way through the mountains on these treks. They were each served a large omelet with cheese and bread, and after sleeping a few hours, they continued their journey, hiking through the rugged peaks of the Dolomites. It was important to move across the border before the Italian troops from Ugovizza came to patrol the area in the morning. The entire journey took two days and one night. After crossing into Italy, the group split up and went their separate ways.

Anna took the train to Udine, where she found a connection to Palmanova. She had previously written her mother to tell her when she was coming, so her mother, Ida, sent Maria to Palmanova to meet her at the train station. Maria was married by now and brought her baby to meet Anna. When Anna saw Maria, she was astonished to see how thin Maria had become. Maria was overjoyed to see Anna again. She was desperately lonely because her husband had been taken as a prisoner of war and had not yet returned home.

Upon reaching her home in Visco, Anna noticed that her mother was also drastically changed. Ida had become withdrawn and no longer cared to socialize with friends. Her appetite was greatly diminished, and she had lost so much weight that her clothes hung loosely upon her. Her hair was unkempt, and her eyes had become vacant and distant. Although Anna tried to lift her spirits, Ida seldom smiled.

Pepi had been trying to engage Ida in conversation, but she had little to say to anyone. He began staying away from home in the evenings and when he did come home, Anna could tell that he had been drinking more wine than he should have. Anna was distressed to see her parents so changed and unhappy. She began the task of running the household even though her parents had become strangers, and she found little joy in being home.

Later that year, Ida began experiencing a great deal of pain, especially in her abdomen, so Anna and Pepi took her to the hospital in Palmanova, where she was diagnosed with liver cancer. She was hospitalized for a month and given morphine for her pain. Pepi stayed silent most of the time and became withdrawn and irritable. His heavy drinking continued, and he spent most of his time away from home. Anna realized it was because he was so sad, but she worried about him because she did not always know where he had gone.

When Ida returned home from the hospital, she would moan and cry out with pain throughout the day and night. She was constantly scratching at herself and complained of itching all over. Anna rubbed her with mentholated oil trying to console her, but Ida was tormented by pain. Anna nursed her day and night.

Each time Ida went to the toilet, she left behind black urine spots in the bed and a strong urine odor. Anna began washing large loads of laundry each day at a little stream near their house where a concrete washboard had been poured years ago. She bathed her mother several times a day to clean and soothe her. She also combed her mother's hair and massaged her throughout the day and at night to help her relax. Anna moved into her parent's room so she could constantly attend to Ida's needs. Pepi began sleeping in Guido's room and distanced himself from their bedroom. During this period, Ann's only ally against sadness and loneliness was Maria and her baby.

That same year, Maria's husband, Signore Tei, returned from the POW camp where he had mistakenly been held as one of Mussolini's troops. Soon after his return, they moved to Perugia, in central Italy, where he had already established a law practice before the war. Anna missed them profoundly and always remembered 1947 as being a miserable year.

In February 1948, Ida Venturini died, not of liver cancer, but of a heart attack while Anna was holding her. After a small service in Santa Maria Maggiore, the local chapel where she had been married, she was buried in the Visco cemetery on Via Dante Alighieri.

Before Ida had passed away, she said that English was going to become an important language and that Anna should continue her language studies. So, after Anna had settled her mother's affairs, she wrote to Giorgio who had been living in London for several years. He invited her to come to London where she could study English and where he could help her find employment.

Anna made sure a local farm family would help care for her father and Guido in exchange for the farm proceeds, so they moved into the house with Pepi and Guido. Anna was happy to be free from the responsibilities of running the house and farm, so she packed her bags and left for London.

Chapter 10
London, England

*A*nna was now twenty-four years old* and filled with enthusiasm and optimism about her future. She wondered what excitement London would hold for her and what it would be like to
spend time with Giorgio again. She hoped he would see her as a
mature, intelligent woman and not the immature child she had
been ten years ago when they first met.

She stepped off the ferry in England and Giorgio was there
to greet her. He looked sophisticated and self-confident. As Anna
studied him, she knew, deep in her heart she truly loved him. She
had played at romance with some of the soldiers in Palmanova,
but no one had come close to measuring up to Giorgio. His deep
laugh lines were permanently carved into his face so even when
relaxed, he still appeared to be smiling. His eyes were bright, and
she could see he was genuinely happy to have her there with him.

They stayed up most of that night exchanging stories, and
she told him about the latest news from Italy. Since he had moved
to London, Giorgio had met many important and high-ranking
contacts through his work as an interpreter. He had also been

commissioned to paint several portraits for wealthy families. Because he enjoyed painting and sketching more than anything else, he hoped one day to paint full time. Giorgio told her about the fabulous parties he had attended and described with great detail the beautiful palaces and large estates he had frequented. He felt that just by being Italian it gave him a cultural advantage in English society. He knew how to use his accent, and the natural animation that Italians have, to intrigue and entertain everyone around him. Italy was, indeed, a favorite destination for English people with the money. Many of those in high society had summer homes in Italy.

For the next several weeks, Giorgio showed Anna around London and introduced her to his friends. He found employment for her as a paid companion to a wealthy widow named, Eleanor. She had a married daughter living far away in northern England and seldom returned to England to visit.

Eleanor was extremely pleased to meet Anna and hired her during their first encounter. Now Anna found herself living in a large, beautiful home in the heart of London. Eleanor had studied German when she was young but had little opportunity to use it before Anna came. She had also been to Trieste several times on her way to Egypt, where her husband's family once owned a large plantation. Anna was like a breath of fresh air in Eleanor's home.

Among her many pursuits, Eleanor liked working on crossword puzzles and playing cards, but she loved for Anna to read to her. Anna selected poetry and stories in several languages, delighting Eleanor with her company and intellect. They practiced Italian, German, and French with each other and discussed many topics and subjects.

Eleanor especially liked studies in philosophy and art. Each day after breakfast, they went for a walk, often to a park or to an art gallery or museum. Many afternoons Eleanor would invite friends to tea and Anna entertained them all. Her last duty each day was to take a cup of warm tea up to Eleanor's room and say goodnight. Eleanor often thanked her for the lovely day which they had spent together making Anna feel genuinely loved and appreciated.

After living with Eleanor for a few months, Anna began taking classes at South Kensington College, majoring in English and secretarial skills which included shorthand. Sometimes in the evenings, or when she had free time, she would meet Giorgio. They went to art galleries, concerts, and other cultural events throughout London together. Anna's feelings for Giorgio deepened and she cherished the times they could be together.

The first time he tenderly kissed her, she let her inhibitions go. No one had ever kissed her so tenderly, and for the first time, she enjoyed love making. Giorgio did not make her feel embarrassed or ashamed when she honestly expressed herself to him. Other men Anna had known in an intimate way had pulled and grabbed at her, forcefully making her do as they wished, often leaving her feeling guilty, unfulfilled, and ashamed. Anna and Giorgio discussed marriage several times but agreed to keep their relationship lighthearted and fun.

Several times, Giorgio invited her to attend elaborate society parties. Women and men alike sought his constant attention. Their clothing was elaborate and fascinating, and Anna had always been interested in fashion. Sometimes she felt a little jealous and uncomfortable with the attention Giorgio gave to the girls who flirted openly with him. They were often very pretty but seemed to be without substance and sometimes snobby toward her which diminished their charms.

Anna had never thought of herself as being beautiful, but these women made her feel inferior and insecure at times at these society parties. She wished that she had more height, wealth, or some sort of title because those things seemed to intrigue these people the most.

To protect her tender emotions, she began spending less time with Giorgio and his friends, and more time at home with Eleanor. Most of Eleanor's friends were elderly and admired Anna for her youthful energy and enthusiasm and her talent for being fluent in several languages. She was the center of attention and always had several dictionaries at her side which she referred to often.

During the second year of living with Eleanor, Anna received a letter from her father in Visco announcing the marriage of Guido to a woman named Iris. Pepi enclosed a picture of Iris which Anna studied. Her first impression was that Iris looked cool and mischievous, yet she was pretty, with a good figure. Anna wondered why Iris would be interested in marrying Guido, but Pepi seemed happy about the marriage, so Anna sent them her best wishes.

One day, while Anna and Eleanor were talking, Eleanor complained of a sudden tiredness that left her so weak she had to sit on a bench to rest. When her breathing became dangerously labored, Anna called out for help. Eleanor was rushed to the hospital where it was determined she had suffered a slight stroke. When she was allowed to come home, she had a full-time nurse to care for her.

After that, Eleanor did not speak much, however Anna continued to read poetry and short essays to her and bring in fresh cut flowers from the garden, which immensely pleased Eleanor.

About a month after coming home from the hospital, Eleanor passed away, while Anna was holding her hand and comforting her through the last minutes of her life. Anna affectionately remembered Eleanor as being a great lady and consoled Eleanor's daughter even though Anna was deeply grieving the loss herself.

She helped settle the estate and found that Eleanor had made provisions in her will for Anna to receive a monetary gift of three hundred pounds. More importantly, Eleanor had left her with a great sense of accomplishment and confidence. Which would serve her well in the future.

Chapter 11
The Duchess

The after-effects of war were still apparent in London in 1951. Ruble from bombed buildings was still lying in the streets and many destroyed roads and bridges had not yet been repaired. People in England were still on food rations. But, thanks to Eleanor, Anna had plenty of money to re-establish herself. Through an advertisement in *The London Times*, she found another position as a paid companion to a duchess. Shortly before Christmas, she moved into the grand quarters of the Duchess de Chateau Thierry at Knights Bridge, near Hyde Park.

During Anna's employment with the duchess, they went on elaborate holidays to France and Spain always staying in beautiful expensive hotels. The duchess also hosted large parties where people with all sorts of titles attended. They gossiped about war spies, and misfortunes of rich friends. Anna noted that the people associated with the duchess seemed much less sincere than the people Eleanor had entertained. However, she continued to be courteous with everyone and, became somewhat of a diplomat, smiling and agreeing with everything anyone had to say.

The duchess also had a dog that was quite old and with a mean temper. It was hard to find anyone willing to take the dog outside for a walk, so Anna took charge of the little dog. The obnoxious little thing barked and growled at anyone who came near and wanted to pet him, while they were out walking. So, Anna decided to set a fast pace each time they went out which eventually wore the little dog down. She also managed to teach the dog some manners, for which the duchess was grateful.

One night, only a few months later, the dog died in its sleep. The duchess was extremely sad about the passing of her little dog and too grief-stricken to make final arrangements, so Anna had to call around to friends of the duchess and ask if they knew of a nice garden where the dog could be properly buried. When no one offered a space for the burial, Anna suggested the dog be buried next to the duchess' son, who had died several years earlier.

"Why, Anna, that is a wonderful idea," the Duchess said, For weeks after the dog's death, guests would come to visit with tokens of their sympathy. It was as if a member of the royal family had died.

Having been rich her entire life, the duchess had no idea how to manage her money or even how much money she had. The Chippendale furniture and the other furnishings in her apartment were exquisite. She had many expensive items from around the world. After the first year she employed Anna, it came as a complete shock to the duchess when she was notified that she was nearly out of money.

As a means of support, the Duchess promised, upon her death, that her Chippendale furniture and expensive collections of art and china would go to certain friends if they loaned her money. Anna was the only one who knew the Duchess accepted money and made promises of her possessions to more than one person.

Nonetheless, in this manner, the Duchess continued to live quite well under these false pretenses.

She had expensive stationery made with her family crest embossed on top of the page and corresponded with many wealthy families throughout Europe. She presented herself with such grace and charm, people continued bringing her fabulous gifts, which she later sold. It was a lucrative way for her to make a substantial living.

Eventually, the duchess was forced to look for a smaller apartment. Anna accompanied her while looking for a suitable residence. The duchess soon realized many people wanted her to rent from them so they could place her name and title in large letters at the entrance hall. Apartments with prestigious residents attracted other wealthy and entitled clients. The landlords were eager to please her.

She could have taken any apartment she wanted but settled on a nice penthouse in a good location near Albert Hall, overlooking Kensington Park.

After establishing herself in her new apartment, the duchess resumed entertaining and throwing great parties which included royal and aristocratic families, ambassadors, and attachés from around the world. The caterers and florists clamored to be involved with her social gatherings. Many businesses willingly donated staff and services to be associated with her and use her name as a reference. The larger the parties became, the more fabulous and expensive were the gifts to her. She graciously accepted them, cataloged, and stored them, until she could arrange to ship them to France where they could be discreetly sold.

Anna's duties with the duchess were light, so to occupy her free time she decided to take several part-time jobs translating newspapers, magazine articles, books, and literature. Because she was fluent in French, Italian, Latin, German, and now English, she had as much work as she wanted. Seldom seeing Giorgio, partially due to their conflicting schedules, she found it amusing that both of them, being country people from northern Italy, had found themselves moving within London's high society.

At the end of her fourth summer in London, Anna received a letter from the family who was caring for her father in Visco. They said her father had fallen off his bike and had broken his leg. He was not in good health, nor in good temperament. They often quarreled with him and asked Anna to return to Italy as soon as possible to take over his care.

After four and a half wonderful years in London, Anna made preparation to return to Italy. The duchess cried when Anna told her she had to leave and told her to come back as soon as she could. Many of the duchess's friends sent notes and small presents to Anna saying how sad they were that she was leaving. One American couple sent her orchids which were rare to find.

Chapter 12
Return to Italy

The day she left London, Anna took a taxi past Giorgio's old apartment, purely for sentimental reasons. He had gone to France with a wealthy English couple who had commissioned him for several paintings of their property, their children, and their pets. Anna was sad to be ending this exciting chapter of her life in London and did not look forward to returning to her family home without her mother being there to greet her.

After taking a ferry from England, she took the long train ride from northern France across the Alps and into Italy. As she crossed the Italian border, she was reminded of how beautiful Italy truly was. She hadn't realized how much she missed the bright blue skies and tall mountains with fresh clear lakes, and green hills. The sun shone bright and warm, and she had a sense of pride about being Italian. Having been in foggy London where even the people could sometimes seem cool and rigid, she laughed at how passionate and animated the Italians were in expressing themselves.

From the train station in Trieste, she walked up the long stone stairway next to the tracks, which led up the steep hill to her Aunt (Tante) Yetta and Cousin Mario's house on Via Trenovia. As she slowly ascended the stairs, she looked back down upon Trieste, the city of her youth, and saw Castello Miramare, the old fish market, and the large hotels on the waterfront. She also noticed new construction throughout the city.

Her Aunt Yetta accepted her with open arms and turned her homecoming into a society event, inviting friends and family from the entire area. Yetta's house was well-kept with a garden full of flowers and rose bushes. During Anna's absence, her cousin, Mario, had become a Doctor of Philosophy, and she found talks with him extremely interesting. She was felt close to her mother being in the house that her grandparents had built in the last century and where her mother had grown up.

After a few days, Anna left the city of Trieste and arrived back home to the small village of Visco. She found her father bedridden and in a cast. The doctor had ordered Pepi to stay in bed for several weeks following his bicycle accident.

Anna found the house dirty, and many things she remembered as being in the house when she left, were now either broken or stolen. Her brother, Guido, was upset and easily confused because his wife, Iris, had recently abandoned him. Vittoria, a nearby farmer's wife had been trying to help run the household, but Pepi, being frustrated, angry, and often drunk was extremely ill-tempered. Their mutual dislike of one another had escalated to a breaking point, so when Anna arrived, Vittoria walked out. This left Anna alone to deal with the responsibilities of running what had become a sad, forlorn home.

Anna learned that Iris had been responsible for much of the distress in their household. She had been nothing more than an opportunist, who had flirted her way into Pepi, and Guido's lives. Being nice-looking, and appearing sincere, she had masked her intentions of establishing herself in the household to eventually inherit the entire property.

Soon after she moved in, Iris had begun selling things from the house. She would pack silver pieces, Ida's jewelry, furs, and whatever she could in a suitcase, and pretend to visit relatives. Then, she would sell the items at the market in another town. Each time she returned home, she had her suitcase filled with new dresses and shoes.

Anna's father, Pepi, said that Iris had become lazy shortly after she and Guido were married. She stopped cooking meals and did not keep the house clean. She would throw tantrums when Guido or Pepi asked her to do anything. Poor Guido gave her whatever she wanted, hoping to restore peace in the household because he craved any attention from her. It was even rumored that she had taken a lover because she was seen with another man in several locations around the area.

When Pepi realized Iris was nothing more than a thief, he reported her to the police for stealing his wife's belongings and household items. Once she found out that Pepi had reported her activities, she began putting small amounts of poison into his food, which was making him sick. If the police had not caught Iris and her lover stealing from another farm, she would have eventually killed Pepi, and possibly even Guido, for the estate.

Anna knew the amount of money she had brought with her from London would soon run out, so she began seeking employment. Because there was no chance of employment in the country around Visco, she would have to look in Trieste. She applied at the American Allied Forces Headquarters as an interpreter, translator, and secretary and was quickly hired with an immediate start date. This was the beginning of her association and career with the Allied Forces now stationed in Italy.

She hired a housekeeper and nurse from Visco to care for her father and brother on weekdays and planned to return to Visco on weekends to manage the household and cook for the week ahead. During the weekdays while in Trieste, she stayed with her Aunt Jetty, and cousin Mario. Aunt Paoula often came to visit them from Dubrovnik. Seeing Ida's sisters together, laughing, talking, and pouring tea, reminded Anna of how much she missed her own mother.

From her aunt's house on the hill above Trieste, they had a magnificent view of the city and harbor below. Her aunt had a large garden full of roses and a fence covered with ivy and morning glories. There were also large bushes of lilacs and pots of geraniums lining the pathways of the flower garden. Along the vegetable garden area, there were flowing fruit trees and a row of assorted flowering plants. The garden was beautiful and peaceful which quieted her soul.

Each day Anna walked to and from work. She took a steep footpath down the hill from her aunt's house on the four hundred-plus stone staircase leading to the center of Trieste and the harbor area where she worked. Sometimes, she took a bouquet of flowers from the garden for her desk.

Working for the Allied Forces pleased her because the staff was orderly, and they treated her well. Working in an English-speaking environment would prove to be a theme throughout the rest of her working life. She was adored by the allied personnel she worked with because of her efficiency, cheerfulness, intelligence, and work ethic. She excelled at her job, even though the major for whom she worked often flirted with her.

He was a handsome man, but also married. She knew she could not let anything develop between them. Anna did not encourage his feelings for her, yet the major continued to ask her to meet him for some "innocent fun." At one point he asked her to go on vacation with him.

This was her first job with military and allied personnel, so it was difficult for her to know how to be friendly towards him yet maintain a professional relationship. She decided to tell him she had been dating an Italian man named Gino which seemed to deter the major's advances towards her.

Gino was tall, slim, well-dressed, and good-mannered. He came from a wealthy family with high social standing in Trieste. He professed his love for Anna on numerous occasions but had an overhearing, jealous mother who tried to control him. She discouraged him from having a serious relationship with Anna. However, they continued to date in secret. Anna had arrived at a point in her life where she felt in control of her life, and had become independent, and emotionally secure.

The following year, the civilian allied employees were told that allied headquarters was moving from Trieste. After ten years of occupation and allied control, this region was being turned over to the Italian government. To retain her position and current pay grade, Anna was now forced to become an employee of the Italian government as a civil servant. They assigned her to the Geophysics Institute as a translator and secretary. The worst thing about her new job was that it was located on the other side of the city and required her to make several bus changes traveling to and from work each day.

Working long hours during the week, she was also required her to work some Saturdays. She found no pleasure in her new position but due to the financial responsibilities for her father and brother, she had to endure the long hours. Her social life suffered, as did her relationship with Gino.

Each weekend Anna returned home to care for her father and Guido. She made the forty-five-kilometer trip from Trieste by train to Palmanova, where she either walked or rode the last three kilometers to Visco by bicycle.

After several months, the long commute became tiresome and wasted too much of her precious free time. Anna decided it would be easier to rent a two-bedroom apartment in Trieste and move her father in with her. She made arrangements with a priest, for Guido to stay at a monastery where he could work as a groundskeeper for part of his board.

Pepi's broken leg had not healed properly and ended up being six inches shorter than his other leg. They arranged for custom-made shoes with a six-inch cork lift which enabled him to walk comfortably. Once adjusted to the move and his new shoe, he liked city life and even helped Anna with a few light household tasks.

Anna continued to see Gino and they took a few nice trips and vacations with other young people. After dating for more than two years, they began to talk seriously about marriage and children and creating a future together. However, Gino's mother did not accept their plans for a serious relationship. She wanted to steer Gino toward other women from wealthier families and took every opportunity to make Anna feel uncomfortable and insecure. Anna realized his mother was selfish and wanted to secure her own financial future through her son.

Adding to Anna's troubles, her half-brother, Dolfi, and the families of her other half-brothers, Piero, and Fedrico, sent a letter from their attorney demanding that she sell the Visco property and divide all assets. Dolfi argued that Ida and his father had built the house and that Pepi had no claim to the property.

Anna now found herself in the middle of a major lawsuit, which drained her time and financial resources. During this period, she became emotionally and physically drained. She was still paying for her father's hospital bills and for Guido's care and she would reflect on this time period as being the worst in her life.

Fortunately, she had a friend who told her about a possible opening at the newly established American Headquarters in Udine which happened to be near Visco. Upon investigation, Anna found that a civilian employment office had been established to hire Italian nationals for the American military headquarters. She submitted her application for employment and was hired as an interpreter. She gladly left work at the Geophysics Institute in Trieste and decided to move back to Visco with her father. Visco was on a direct bus line to Udine and her commute would be short. Since Anna and Pepi would be living in the house again; her brothers could not make her sell the Visco house.

Chapter 13
Working for the Americans - Udine

*A**nna began working at the American headquarters** in Udine on January 6, 1956, Epiphany Day of the Three Kings. She felt as if she, herself, had been given wonderful presents: a new job, a better life, and a promising future. She was thankful to have a job working for the Americans, in which she could use her English language skills. How insightful her mother had been when telling her to learn English. At that time, many people in Italy were unhappy, unemployed, and had few language skills, beyond Italian, or German.

Each day, on her way to work, Anna went into town to a nearby pastry shop and bought sweets for the morning meetings. A local café would send cappuccinos. It was an enjoyable way to start the day because once work started, there was little time for socialization.

She was assigned to work for two men: Director of Materials and the Information officer. Each day she was given Italian newspapers to translate into English; the articles usually reported on American Air Force personnel. Her bosses were impressed by her intellect and the quality of her translations. She was happy to be making a small contribution to the largest most power military organization in the world.

Anna sometimes wondered about the qualifications of the Information Officer because his mind constantly wandered. She thought he was like a puzzle that had not been put together properly. One day, an article she had translated said that this officer had been in a bar fight the previous night. When he arrived at work that morning, his face was bruised, his nose appeared to be broken and one of his eyes was swollen nearly shut. He confided to Anna that he had been fighting over an Italian girl from Trieste, and that he felt torn between his responsibilities back in the United States and his feelings for this Italian girl.

Later, when summoned by the Colonel, he lied and said he had met some communists in a bar, and they beat him up because he was an American. A formal investigation followed, and when it was found there were no communists involved just that he had been drunk and disorderly, he was sent back to the United States to join his family. Anna had liked him and felt sorry for him.

***

The American Headquarters was located in a large palace, situated in the center of Udine, just around the corner from Anna's bus stop, which was very convenient. Anna left Visco each morning at 6:30 a.m. to catch the bus and arrive at work on time. The headquarters had been set up with central heating on two floors of the oldest and most elegant palace in Udine. The Italians, being more conservative, kept the building temperature low. The Americans, however, were much more extravagant and liked the heat going full blast. During the severe cold of February, with continuous snowstorms, the boiler started failing and eventually quit.

After that there were only small electric stoves to keep the huge, drafty space comfortable enough to continue working there.

On the first floor were the offices of the Commander, Information Officer, Military Personnel, Civil Engineering and Drafting department. The entire second floor was devoted to the Civilian Personnel office. From there, a narrow staircase led up to the Judge Advocate and Finance offices on the third floor.

The palace had a large imposing marble staircase off the center of the foyer leading to the second floor. Anna's desk was situated on the first floor just off the main foyer and she could see the constant movement up and down the staircase. She enjoyed studying people and their interactions. Some people walked gracefully up or down the stairs softly and slowly while smiling at people as they passed. Others tromped up or down the staircase loudly and some looked straight ahead or walked with their eyes cast downward. There were people who stopped to chat and flirt. Some even proposing outings or making dates. It was an innocent place to meet and pause for a short time, or to brush against them slightly whether intended or not.

Most importantly, she could see the Italians and Americans were adjusting to one another it was as if they were actors on a grand stage. An elegant staircase upon which many stories started and ended.

A large ballroom had been converted into offices by using screens to separate work areas. The walls and ceiling of the ballroom were decorated with beautifully painted Frescos. One large painting represented the loveliest dawn Anna could image; soft pink clouds surrounded a tender shepherd scene. It was a nice place for Anna to pause during her regular, and frequent trips, to other offices delivering or collecting papers.

***

Most of the time airmen were cheerful and fun loving, but right before an inspection everyone seemed caught up in a whirlwind of stress with the extra duties and correcting procedural discrepancies. Anna had to help research the manuals and make sure everything was updated and filed into proper sections of the manuals, prior to the inspections. Constant procedural changes were made, but filing the extra paperwork was almost a fulltime job. Unfortunately, it would pile up a bit between sections because there simply was not enough time or help to do everything each day.

She noted the American soldiers represented many races and religions and were from diverse backgrounds and geographic locations. It was remarkable that all these soldiers had a genuine sense of pride in being "American," Anna could sense this through their enthusiasm. *It must be a great country,* she thought, as she compared it to Italy and how divided and distant the regions all seemed to be.

Anna was amazed to see how many American soldiers were taller and more robust than the Italians. This made her aware of how small she really was. Once a major came into the office and saw her struggling to reach a top shelf.

"How tall are you, Anna?"

Looking meekly up at him, she answered: "Almost five feet."

"Yes, *almost,*" he replied. They both had a good laugh and, from then on, he placed correspondence to be typed on a lower shelf for her.

Another challenge for Anna was trying to put away or pull files from the top drawers of tall filing cabinets. Eventually, she solved this problem by bringing in a little wooden stool which her father had made for her as a child.

Always friendly, outgoing, and efficient, Anna received many compliments from the men thanking her for her work. Trying to stay upbeat and enthusiastic, she realized many of them were sad and lonely, missing their families and friends back in the United States.

***

The first real crush she felt for an American soldier, was for a staff sergeant from Special Services. Her imagination caused her to blush when he came anywhere near. Handsome, tall, and slender, he had blue eyes and dark hair. He walked so softly, she often could not hear him coming until he would suddenly appear and startle her. Noticing her reaction, he told her he was an American Indian and that walking softly was an ancestral trait of his.

How extraordinary, she thought, and liked to study him when he wasn't looking. If she would have let herself go, she could have fallen very much in love with him. But she was still tied down with family troubles and there was no time for romantic intrigues.

***

In addition to the headquarters in Udine, where Anna worked, the Americans occupied a few offices in Campoformido, an old Italian airfield near Udine that had been used to train Italian pilots for the Tricolore, an Italian national acrobatic flying team. They flew with the colors of Italy: green, white, and red smoke stretching evenly after the planes as they demonstrated their flying abilities.

The American military also had offices in a small Italian airfield near Aviano, a small village at the base of the Dolomite mountains about ninety kilometers southwest of Udine. Staff cars frequently ran between these three locations. therefore, much time was lost during these commutes. Therefore, the Commander decided to find a location with enough airfield possibilities to expand and consolidate all three military sites, into one base of operations. Anna was asked to be interpreter and guide for the headquarters commander, and his staff, when they made the trip to Aviano to see if the area would be able to support a new base.

Driving toward Aviano they could see *Piancavallo*, the tallest peak in the region rising above the flat plains upon which the tiny village of Aviano was located. Pordenone was the largest city near Aviano, located only fifteen kilometers away, and was the commercial center for the region. It was decided Pordenone would serve nicely as a support community for the large influx of American troops expected to arrive once an airbase was established there in northern Italy.

Based on his geographical and economic impact reports, the commander decided to move the headquarters from Udine to Aviano. There was plenty of space in the countryside for improvements and to enlarge the existing airfield to accommodate American jets and cargo planes. Aviano held another great strategic advantage by being only two minutes airtime from the communist Yugoslavian border.

That is how the small Italian airfield became the American Air Force Base of Aviano in 1957.

***

The quaint little village of Aviano, in the province of Pordenone, Italy, was now transformed into a noisy, bustling North Atlantic Treaty Organization (NATO) base. Most of the time, a good sense of humor existed between the soldiers and Italian civilians, but some locals protested the Americans being there and taking over the area. Others were happy to see the area prosper. The local markets grew and the housing and building industry employed people from all over the region. Many dirt roads were paved, and businesses sprang up everywhere offering services to

American soldiers and their families, taking advantage of the booming economy.

Anna did not accept this change to a new location with a light heart; but because unemployment in Italy was high at that time, and her salary was good with excellent benefits, she was compelled to move near Aviano to keep her position. She rented a room above a trattoria in Roveredo. Once again, she made arrangements for the care of her father, Pepi, and for Guido's care in Visco. Anna and Gino's relationship slowly dissolved. A few years afterwards, her aunt from Trieste sent her a newspaper clipping announcing Gino's engagement to a wealthy socialite in Trieste.

***

Aviano skies were soon filled with large cargo planes and jets practicing maneuvers. They split the sky with such speed and agility one did not see the jets coming until after they had flown past. The delayed sound shook all sides of the old metal hangers located along the runways which housed the supply and flight support offices, long after the jets had passed. When large cargo planes landed and took off, Anna could feel deep vibrations from the ground up through her entire body.

The opposite side of the hanger faced the rocky gray Dolomites and green foothills of the plains. The mountains stood majestic and peaceful. Some days, they would be wrapped in thin ribbons of fog; other days their heads were hidden in the haze. When the air was clear, the ever-changing colors of the clouds seemed more intense. Through much of the year the mountain crevasses hid snow and frost from the sun. The bold, bare face of the mountain seemed wrinkled by the harsh winter weather. In the summer, dark patches of trees called out for visitors to come rest in the shade on the hot days. Viewing the mountains gave Anna a sense of peace and balance that the flight line jets took away.

When alerts and maneuvers were not being practiced by the jets, and when other planes were not landing or taking off, the base returned to the harmonious sounds of nature and the nearby countryside farms.

***

Anna and the other bilingual secretaries and interpreters from the Military Personnel Office at Base Headquarters were extremely busy making contacts with the local Italians. They helped settle disputes, write letters, translate laws and official documents. Anna often brought work home because there was too much to do during officer hours.

One of the jobs she found most challenging was writing and typing the Effectiveness Reports because many of her supervisors lacked good writing skills. They didn't always use proper grammar or vocabulary and would ask her to write and rewrite many official correspondences, then after they approved the drafts, she would retype. Often when the document was perfectly typed and spaced, ready for the final signature her supervisor would cross out or add a word or even a comma, which would ruin the integrity of the document making her type it all over again.

Some evenings she would stay late just to get caught up on her typing. During the day, the phone rang constantly and there were always people coming into the office interrupting her work. She invested in the best English dictionary available, and it never left her side. Soon, she became an expert in English grammar and usage. *Ironic*, she thought, *now they pay me to learn English, and just a few years ago I was learning English myself!*

Another major hindrance to her job was the high turnover rate of her supervisors. It seemed just as she became familiar with a new supervisor's style and needs, a new supervisor would be assigned. With each new supervisor came new changes. The offices and desks were rearranged, and sometimes the walls were repainted. Anna was expected to help take on these new tasks in addition to meeting all the deadlines of her secretarial job.

Physical changes to the work environment were easier to adapt to than the emotional changes she experienced. She had to adjust her feelings of loss each time a dear friend left the office.

The new orders would come to Anna's desk, and she would hand them out, putting on a brave face, she always smiled and wished them well. Then she would start mentally preparing herself for the day they would leave. Usually, she was also responsible for organizing a farewell party.

Of course, the person leaving was usually happy and excited about going back home to the U.S. They would talk at length about their hometowns and where they came from. Fortunately, their orders came with at least 90 days' notice which gave everyone time to prepare for their departure.

Chapter 14
Aviano Air Force Base

*A*nna shared a room in Roveredo with another Italian girl from Trieste named Milena. Anna was happy for Milena's company because she felt lonely at times and missed her aunt and the social activity of Trieste.

Milena worked in Military Personnel at the Aviana Air force Base with Anna and liked to flirt with the American soldiers. Being a beautiful, tall, slender blonde, the soldiers enjoyed flirting back. Milena was somewhat selective in her flirtations because she was really shopping for a husband. Anna, on the other hand, did not encourage men to flirt with her because she had enough problems already.

During the week, Anna and Milena would entertain themselves by reading, writing, and studying. Their only social interaction outside of work was at the trattoria, located on the main floor of where they stayed. Sometimes they would rent bikes and go shopping in Pordenone after work. It was amazing that a small bike could give them a such a sense of freedom and pleasure. Milena eventually found a boyfriend who would take her anywhere she wanted to go, so she began attending many Base functions and parties.

Anna continued to ride her bike increasingly more and even started to commute to and from work by bike when the weather was nice. It was easy to catch a ride with one of the Americans going to the Base when the weather was bad.

One of the officers who often gave Anna a ride, wanted to explore sites for recreational facilities to be used by people stationed at Aviano A.F.B. He asked her to serve as his interpreter while he scouted facilities throughout northern Italy. They took several day trips and Anna was excited to be out of the office. It was a joy for her to be touring the countryside in this officer's beautiful blue Chevrolet.

On one occasion, however, he traveled down a road that became too narrow for his car to pass. The Italians yelled obscenities at him, which Anna did not translate. She felt totally relaxed and at ease with him and was thankful he never made advances toward her or displayed any inappropriate behavior.

On one particular outing, they went to check out a golf course near Vittorio Veneto. The only other golf courses were four hours' drive away near Florence. The Count Ugolino course in Florence was one of the most exclusive clubs in Italy. It became a popular destination for officers on weekends and was often used as a recruiting tool for new officers. Anna and the officer's friendship continued long after he was stationed back in the U.S.

***

Newly arriving airmen were always advised to leave their American cars back home in the United States and buy a smaller European car upon their arrival in Italy. On major highways, the large American car was a dream to ride in, but in small villages and on tiny winding roads, a large car was impractical.

The narrow roads in Italy were ancient, originally built for donkey carts, carriages, and farm wagons, and did not accommodate huge American cars well. Still, there were some who didn't heed the advice and shipped their cars to Italy anyway. Many turns were too tight and Italian buildings were too close together to drive between them. What a commotion was created when the American cars became stuck on the road.

***

On days when Anna stayed in the office, one of her responsibilities was to type welcome letters to newly assigned personnel. Following is a copy of one letter which demonstrates how complicated and difficult the first trip to Aviano was for them.

Welcome to Aviano

"When precise information about your arrival date and time is known, your assigned sponsor will meet you at the Pordenone train station. Your sponsor will be an established resident of Aviano Air Force base. This "buddy system" is designed to help you get settled and adjusted to your new assignment here in Northern Italy.

"You will stay at the Moderno Hotel in Pordenone for the first night. Should a mix-up in travel schedules occur, upon arriving at the Pordenone train station you are to take a taxi to the Moderno Hotel. This hotel houses both income and department personnel, and the hotel staff will help you make contact with someone at the base.

"If you arrive during duty hours Monday through Friday, 0800-1700 hours, and Saturday 0900-1200 hours, telephone Aviano Air Base from the hotel and ask for extension 340. You will get further instructions, and all preparations will be made for your processing in person. If you are unable to secure hotel

accommodations and it is after-duty hours, contact the Officer of the Day at the Air Base. He will give you assistance in finding transportation and hotel rooms.

Don't blame the cartographers if you can't find Aviano on your handy home map of the world! Aviano is often uncharted on maps. It is a very small village in northern Italy at the foot of the Italian Alps. Find the halfway point between Venice and Trieste on the Adriatic coast. Go north about 70 miles and you'll be able to pinpoint the area around Aviano.

"So, you've never been to Italy? Sure, you saw "three Coins in a Fountain" and "Summertime", you eat pizza fairly regularly, and your wife likes painted Italian shoes (fashionable at the time), but not until orders arrived assigning you to Aviano Air Base, Italy, did you ever think about living in the land of Pompei, the Colosseum, and the Gondolas from Venice.

"If you are typical of the great majority of Air Force personnel traveling to Italy, you'll depart by air from McGuire Air Force Base, New Jersey. You will land at Rhein Main Air Base near Frankfurt, Germany. You will then transfer to a commercial airline from a flight to either Milan, Italy, or to Treviso, which is closer to Aviano. The entire trip should take from two to three days.

"Before departing Frankfurt, purchase L5,000 from the American Express office in the PAX terminal. When you land at Malpensa Airport in Milano, present a copy of your orders to the commercial flight desk (TWA, Alitalia) to get a ticket for the long bus ride into Milan. From the downtown airline office, telephone the Military Railway Transportation office at the Milano Railroad station. The RTO will arrange your taxi transportation to the station and ticketing on to Aviano by rail.

"Should you arrive at Treviso, the airport personnel will take you to the train station. There you will be required to *exchange your travel warrant at the ticket window and board the first train going to Pordenone for a ride approximately an hour long.*

"Anna and Luigi are Italian employees who work at the Aviano Personnel Office. Send them a letter with all of your questions. They have watched 395 American families settle with 1021 dependents in and around the Aviano area. They know that every question that is answered before a family leaves the United States is worth its weight in Michelangelo statutes."

Anna was one of the first Italian employees that the new airmen and their families met when they arrived. She listened patiently to their stories and tried to make light of any difficulties as much as she could. She tried putting them at ease and charmed them with her smile and enthusiasm, reassuring them that Aviano was a wonderful placed to be stationed.

Travel arrangements became easier as more people were assigned to Aviano. Anna was astonished to see how many military families actually made it on or near their arrival dates, however, most people arrived confused and exhausted. Those pioneers had many stories to tell about missed planes, buses, trains, and connections due to severe weather and the lack of communication.

***

In the fall, as usual, with early darkness, came a cold dampness from the Adriatic coast. During long evenings, Anna and her roommate, Milena, lingered near the cooking fires in the main kitchen of the trattoria. The sleeping rooms above the store were hard to heat and often uncomfortably cold. When they retired to their room at night, Anna and Milena often brought candles with them to read by. They shared a large bed with a warm down comforter that kept them cozy and comfortable throughout the night.

A severe flu epidemic hit the area that winter, and Milena became miserably ill. Anna was afraid she would catch the flu from Milena and knew she could not afford to be ill because she absolutely had to go to home to Visco each weekend. As a precaution, she took the advice an old lady had once given her, which was to gargle each more with a small glass of *grappa* (a strong alcoholic liquor). This home remedy burned her lips and gums and made her choke, but she did not get the flu that year. Maybe it was the *grappa* or, maybe it was a miracle, but Anna did not fall ill that winter!

When the weather broke in springtime, Anna and Milena hitched a ride to Pordenone to see a circus. By the time the performances ended, they had missed the last bus back to Roveredo. Luckily, the zoo's animal trainer offered to give them a lift. His truck had a horrible smell from the animals he worked with, but he was talkative and friendly. The girls were friendly and polite, but when they didn't invite him up to their room at the *trattoria*, he looked disappointed and openly pouted to play on their sympathy. His "acting" amused them, and they leapt out of his truck waving good-bye. Long after they left him that evening, the animal smell of his truck stayed with them.

***

One day, a young F-100 pilot came to Aviano for a three-month tour. The first time Milena saw him, he was driving a Mercedes 300 with the door that lifted upward, she immediately set her sights on him the minute they were introduced. When they began dating, Milena became energized. Almost every evening she went out to eat, drink or dance with her new pilot friend.

Anna, herself, had no time for a social life and was content to be working on base and interacting with the Americans during the day. Everyone was polite and treated her with kindness and respect. She found her work to be interesting and had a wide variety of duties from several of the offices. She typed and translated documents and letters for the departments and was also asked to type letters for the American elementary school system. In addition to her typing assignments, she assisted in settling housing issues, police disputes, and served as an interpreter for the constant misunderstandings between Italian landlords and their American renters.

Sometimes Anna would accompany military personnel to the American Consulate in Trieste, transporting classified documents. Usually, several people were in the car with them, all going to conduct official business in Trieste.

Frequently, they took the scenic highway along the coast to Trieste, sometimes stopping at a restaurant on the way back to the base. Most Americans were enthusiastic about being in Italy, she enjoyed and eagerly answered their numerous questions about Italian life. Anna was caught up in their optimistic zest for life and often received praise for her own enthusiastic nature.

Having little free time, Anna had to often decline invitations to parties and dinners in American homes and continued going home to Visco on weekends to do laundry and keep house for her father and Guido on weekends.

***

Milena's boyfriend, the pilot, was gone for three months, but suddenly returned and asked her to marry him. Anna was invited to the wedding, which was held in Trieste. Milena's new husband flew back to the United States with his squadron soon after the wedding, and Milena went by ship, entering the U.S. through the Port of New Orleans. Anna wondered if Milena and her new husband were really well-suited for each other because she had seen many quarrels between them while they were dating.

He had been married and divorced before, which left him with a few legal problems and complications. However, Milena had dreamed of marrying an American pilot so, under these circumstances, Anna bid them farewell and good luck.

***

Anna decided to rent a two-bedroom apartment in Pordenone so she could move her father in with her. Commuting to Visco to maintain the house and care for her father had become too time-consuming and had exhausted her.

When it was time to move her father to Pordenone, her supervisor, Colonel Moore, offered to bring his big American car and help her. Anna's father was still unable to walk very well, so Colonel Moore was kind enough to carry him to the car. After they arrived in Pordenone, the Colonel carried Pepi up many stairs into Anna's new apartment. Anna was thankful for his kindness and support.

She continued to be preoccupied about her father's health and hired a lady to care for him during the day; but Pepi was careless with his smoking habit and continued to drink a considerable amount of wine daily. He became verbally abusive to the woman and was sometimes destructive. Anna sympathized with both of them, but between working all day, shopping for groceries, cooking, cleaning, washing, and going to the doctors for her father's medicines, she had little time to dwell on their complaints.

Chapter 15
Health Problems Arise

*I*n *mid-summer of 1957,* Anna began experiencing pain in her lower abdomen. After the pain persisted for several weeks, she decided to see a doctor in Visco. He directed her to the hospital in Palmanova where she was told she needed her appendix removed. Since she worked in the office of Personnel Affairs, Anna prepared her own paperwork for a medical leave. Then, she was admitted to the hospital in Palmanova and remained there for a week.

While recuperating, she received a great deal of concern and kindness from her many friends and co-workers at the base. The outpouring of emotions surprised her, and she thought how exceptionally thoughtful they were.

It took another two weeks for Anna to recover. Even though she still felt tired and ill at times, she returned to work at Aviano Air Base. One night she found herself again in a great deal of pain. She went to bed thinking she would feel better in the morning, but later that night she had an attack of acute abdominal pain and a high fever and had to be taken to the hospital in Udine.

For seventeen days she was unable to eat, while they took x-rays and blood tests. After finding kidney stones, the doctors decided to operate and remove the stones, which kept her in the hospital for another two weeks. She felt terrible about missing work again, but several people from the Base came to visit and reassured Anna at the hospital. Even Colonel King, commander of the Base came to express his concern for her.

Anna went back home to Visco to recuperate, Giovanna, a local farm woman volunteered to look after her. Giovanna was grateful for the opportunity to care for Anna because, years ago, Anna's mother, Ida, had taken care of Giovanna's family when they were nearly destitute and in need of employment.

When Anna was ready to return to work. Her supervisor from the base came with several of his children to bring her back to Pordenone. When Anna returned to work, people in her office brought in wine, cheese, and flowers to welcome her back.

Captain and Mrs. Shepherd became two of her dearest friends. When he was hired as the Special Services Director, Mrs. Shepherd wanted to learn Italian, so Anna went to their home once a week to teach her conversational Italian. Sometimes Anna would be invited to stay for supper. She enjoyed helping prepare the food and learned a great deal about the culture of the Appalachian Mountains of West Virginia where the Shepherds had lived.

Mrs. Shepherd was a woman of many cultural interests and had a devotion to the great Italian painters. The Shepherds had three sons and in evenings when everyone was home together, they played magnificent records. Even the sons joined in sometimes when they danced and hopped to the music. Anna loved the time spent with this wonderful family.

Mrs. Shepherd and Anna went on several excursions to Florence and Volterra to visit art galleries and buy alabaster and other fine works of art. Mrs. Shepherd especially liked the delicate art of *intarsio* (inlaid pieces of wood or marble placed to form pictures or symbols) and bought many nice pieces to take back to West Virginia.

When Mr. Shepherd's assignment was over and they returned to the United States, Anna felt a deep loneliness for them.

***

As time went by, an official Special Services Department was developed at the Base. A black lieutenant arrived as the Director of Personnel services. This was the first time Anna had worked for a black man. He introduced several intramural sports to Aviano A.F.B. and arranged games with local Italian teams. He traveled much of the time and after each trip he would bring all the secretaries in his office a small gift. He kept himself in good condition, and everyone admired him for his kindness and enthusiasm for sports, recreation, and fitness.

Within a short time, the new director arranged for a swimming pool to be built and established a new recreation center. As part of the Recreation Center, a Touring Office was created so that military servicemen and their families could be easily assisted in making travel plans. Anna helped arrange tours around Italy, Germany, Switzerland, Austria, and France, and served as a tour guide on many occasions. She was uniquely qualified for this position because of her working knowledge of German, French, Italian and English.

***

In addition to working at the Touring Office, Anna helped write and publish the first pamphlet which served as an introduction to the area for the newly assigned personnel to Aviano. An elementary school had been established on the Base, but on Sunday afternoons, high school students had to be bused away to an Army post in Vicenza. The students would remain in Vicenza until Friday afternoon when they were bused back home to Aviano.

These transportation arrangements and separations destressed many families. Anna did her best to console them and worked diligently with the Commander to establish a high school at Aviano Air Force Base.

***

After the personnel director left, the next director arrived, and he too became a good friend. He was musically inclined and asked Anna to accompany him to Padova, as a translator, to procure musical instruments for the Base. He set up several music studios for practices and organized dance lessons at the Recreation Center. Many people signed up for lessons and the program was a great success. Anna had always been a good dancer, and very much enjoyed being a part of this program. She learned the Cha Cha and how to dance the Rumba and the Fox Trot, but Anna regretted not having time to learn the Boogie-Woogie. She found dancing to be good exercise for her mind, body, and spirit. Everyone went home from the lessons happy and light- hearted. These were some of her happiest days spent working at the base.

Her supervisor added much gaiety to the festivities at the Base, however, she felt sorry for him because, even though he was a devoted husband, his wife had left him because she did not like living in Italy and had returned to the United States to be with her own family. Anna often felt like he tried to cover up his sadness with music. During the time they worked together they developed a great respect and understanding for one another.

***

The Italian Air Force Base at Campoformido decided to hold an air show to demonstrate the unique stunts of the Italian Tricolori Acrobatic Team. They invited some American dignitaries and Anna was asked to accompany them as one of the interpreters. The party was a grand, elaborate affair and was held at the Officer's Club.

The name cards and place setting were arranged so that each American couple would be seated next to an Italian couple. A bi-lingual interpreter sat between each couple. All couples were excited and fascinated with the differences and similarities between the two cultures. They exchanged ideas and asked questions, and when the conversation seemed to move too slowly, Anna would say something to stimulate the conversation. She was constantly laughing and smiling and encouraging each of the couples to try to speak a few words from each other's languages.

After dinner was served, the music started, and dancing began on the patio. Anna danced with many nice Americans and Italian officers and at midnight, one of the captains accompanied her home. She would remember this as one of the grandest evenings of her life.

***

There were times Anna missed not being married. She would have liked a lifelong companion and children of her own but considered herself too old by this time to start a romantic relationship.

Giorgio had been her one true love, but they had drifted apart. She received a letter from a friend of his telling her that Giorgio had died from a sudden heart attack.

Nearly all her friends were married. When they complained to her about the troubles of being married, and responsibilities of running a household without any appreciation, she understood them completely. She herself had all the work and responsibility of running a household for many years with none of the fun or status of being married.

By now, Anna realized the importance of having reliable transportation and decided to take driving lessons so by December of 1961, she had her first driver's license. Then, she bought her first car, a Fiat 500, from an American sergeant. It was inexpensive but did not run well, plus she later discovered the gas gauge was broken. On more than one occasion she found herself out of gas or broken down on the side of the road. The sergeant agreed to buy back the car.

Her second car was a black and red Bianchina Spider with nice chrome accents. Some people called Anna "Speedy Gonzales" after a popular song at that time.

Anna's new car
a black and red Bianchina Spider
1961

When her father fell a second time, breaking his thigh bone, he had to be placed in a body cast. His new condition put a terrible strain on the couple who was caring for him. He became louder and demanding, and they complained to Anna constantly. Before Anna could make arrangements for someone else to care for her father, they left. She then hired an old woman willing to care for him, who was not completely of sound mind, but for now, Anna decided that she would have to do! The stress of trying to hold everything together gave her terrible migraines and she still did not feel altogether well herself.

Anna knew her father was depressed because she could see the light in his eyes diminishing little by little. She also sensed that he longed for the quiet countryside and the country house in Visco.

To try and boost his spirits, Anna decided to resign from the Air Force Base and take him back to Visco. Perhaps she could find work at a new Italian industry plant at Torviscosa, only nine kilometers from Visco. With a heavy heart she decided to leave work at Aviano and apply for a job in Torviscosa, as a secretary and Interpreter.

Over time, her father's health deteriorated. He continued drinking and would drift off to sleep for long periods of time. When he woke up, he would yell and demand more wine, drinking again until he passed out. He was admitted to the hospital in Palmanova, and on March 12, 1962, Pepi died at the hospital from liver disease.

Anna sold some of the farmland to pay for her father's hospital and medical bills. She made repairs to the house and garden and continued to work in Torviscosa as an interpreter, using her French, English and German language skills to translate documents.

She was paid a monthly salary, not an hour wage like she had been paid at the Air Force base. She worked long hours and her supervisors in Torviscosa were cool and distant. They expected Anna and the rest of the office staff to stay at work until after 8:00 p.m. sometimes. On a few occasions she had to stay until eleven o'clock in the evening to complete her work.

After having worked for the Americans, she had grown accustomed to better working conditions. She went to the supervisor in charge of Personnel and told him she could not work under these conditions any longer and that many of the other staff felt the same way. After six months of work there, she picked up a bouquet of flowers from her desk and waved good-bye to the industry plant in Torviscosa.

***

The previous year, before Anna had left Aviano Air Force Base, the Director of Personnel had told her to come back whenever she could, and that he would be glad to rehire her. Now, she contacted him and the next day the secretary in the Personnel Office called her back to offer her another job, at the Aviano Air Force Base working for the 40th Supply Squadron.

She found a nice room for rent with a lovely German/Italian family in Pordenone. Ilse was a German War Bride married to Ruggero, an Italian soldier. They had three sweet, polite, well-behaved children and Anna would remain in their home during the weekdays for the next thirteen years. They celebrated holidays with German traditions and songs Anna remembered from her own childhood. During the time Anna lived with the family, they had a beautiful new baby girl and named her, Chiarra, who became Anna's Godchild and always held a special place in her heart.

***

Anna happily returned to familiar surroundings of the Aviano Air Base and was welcomed back as if she were a returning war hero. She was hired as a secretary for the Chief of Supply. His office was combined with the Central Administration office and the Management and Procedures office. Francesca, another Italian secretary, and Anna were both hard working and serious minded and ran an efficient office.

Anna thrived in the friendly atmosphere of the base. What a contrast this office was compared to the Italian industry job she had just left.

Chapter 16
Decade of Harmony

*A*nna *was now 48 years old and entered a period of harmony.* She felt her health had been restored and she was optimistic about life's opportunities. She was content and felt appreciated at work and continued to meet many new Americans as the air base began to increase in size and in personnel.

In August 1970, she was invited to an American BBQ and picnic on base. For the first time, she saw the people she worked with every day now dressed in civilian clothing. The American-stye was casual, comfortable, and practical. A large barbeque grill was set up and there was an abundance of food and wine, all served with the spirit of generosity and fellowship. Because it was the weekend, the military base was peaceful, except for an occasional F-104 Jet that touched down. The war in Vietnam was far away and it was as if nothing bad could happen on such a beautiful day.

By January 1972, Anna was still working at the 40th supply squadron on the flight line when AIC Alice (Allyson) Murlin arrived to work in Anna's section. Allyson was the first single

Woman in the Air Force (WAF) to be assigned to Aviano Air Force Base. What a commotion she caused, not only in Anna's office, but on the entire base. Tall, with red hair, Allyson had a friendly, outgoing personality which Anna liked very much. She nicknamed her "Rita" after Rita Hayworth, the Hollywood actress, because when Allyson entered the office, all work seemed to stop. Everyone wanted her attention, and the Italians were curious and intrigued to see a woman soldier.

Anna was thirty years older than Allyson, and nearly two feet shorter, but they were to become great friends and traveling companions for the rest of Anna's life.

In July, that same year, Anna held a party for about fifty people at her home in Visco to celebrate St. Anna's Day and celebrate the restoration of her house. She decorated the yard with Venetian lights on a rope and had carved out decorative cabbages with candles lining the walkway. There were ten chickens roasting on an open pit, and a nicely decorated table in the yard where she placed olives, mushrooms and peaches soaked in a bowl of good red wine accompanied with a variety of cakes. A big wooden tub was filled with large ice blocks and cold water to keep large slices of watermelon cool.

Many Americans and Italians from the Base along with a few local families attended. Two Italian friends of hers who worked at the Base, Lia, and Francesca, came in Francesca's tiny car. Somehow, they also managed to squeeze two American pilots into the car with them. These pilots had crowded into the back seat, but their long legs had to be left hanging out of the car. It was a spectacle that gave everyone a great laugh.

It was a wonderful party with music and dancing throughout most of the night. Some of the Americans talked about starting a baseball league, in which Italian teams would play against the American servicemen at Aviano. The last guests left Anna's party at about six a.m. the next morning.

The following year in January, Anna went to Belluno to see a specialist for a new pain she had begun experiencing in her lower back. Soon afterward, she was hospitalized for three months this time and had more kidney stones removed. It took a long time to recover from this latest operation and she did not feel well for the entire summer.

That fall, her friend, Allyson, returned to the United States and was deeply missed. But both women promised to keep in contact and see each other again.

***

Now Anna decided to take an apartment in Pordenone at Via Marconi, No. 4, near the old City Center. One of her good friends, Hilda, who had worked with Anna at the base, knew about a beautiful apartment when it became available in her building.

Already good friends, Anna and Hilda found it comforting to be living so near one another. It was at this time Anna received word from the priest in Visco that her brother, Guido, had passed away from a sudden heart attack.

***

The next year, Allyson returned for a second tour of duty at Aviano. Anna met her on the flight line with a bouquet of roses as she stepped off the plane. The office where they had worked together threw a "Welcome Back" party for Allyson, and many people who had known her from the previous year flooded the room in a festive mood. Anna and Allyson renewed their friendship and began taking trips to markets in Visco, Trieste, Portogruaro, and to historical sites.

In 1976, Allyson's mother, Elizabeth, came from the United States to visit and Anna invited them to a grand luncheon at her apartment in Pordenone. They all took short one-day trips around northeastern Italy together, talking about history and art.

On the last day of Elizabeth's visit, May 6, 1976, a devastating earthquake hit the entire region. About nine o'clock that evening, the first large tremor shook all of the houses and apartment buildings. There were smaller tremors throughout the night, but other than several cracks in her walls the following morning, it appeared there was no other significant damage to Anna's apartment.

The epicenter was about sixty kilometers away near a small town at the base of the Dolomites, called Gemona, which was completely destroyed. Many of the small villages in northwestern Italy were reduced to rubble.

Numerous countries offered aid and sent troops to help set up tents and distribute food, water, and clothing to the displaced Italian families in the region. Americans at the base immediately sent crews and equipment to the most devastated areas. They also sent the base minister and priest to help comfort thousands of people left homeless by the earthquake.

In a letter regarding the entire event, Anna wrote:

"I personally have been long enough with American soldiers as a civilian to testify that the Americans are the best people on earth. After all, America was formed by people from all over the world. They built a new country by helping each other. BLESSED BE AMERICA for being so quick to respond to our dire needs."

***

In 1978, Anna's Aunt (*zia*) Jetti from Trieste died suddenly, leaving her elderly son, Mario, alone in the large house at Via Trenovia, where Anna's grandparents had lived. Anna continued living in Pordenone and working at Aviano Air Base during the week. However, she now started going to Trieste each weekend to care for her cousin, Mario, and help him with cooking and household chores. She enjoyed being in her mother's childhood home again and looked forward to weekends and holidays which she could spend time there with Mario. He was an intellectual and held a doctorate degree in Philosophy and Medicine. Anna enjoyed having deep, thought-provoking conversations and debates with him, and felt they both learned much from each other.

Anna had many fond memories associated with her grandparent's house on Via Trenovia. Each side of the house had a balcony with the largest, most elaborate balcony overlooking the city port of Trieste and the Adriatic coast. Anna could see many fine villas and gardens cascading below from the balcony because the house was situated high on a hill overlooking them all. She and Mario would sit on the front balcony facing the sea and watch the boats, steamers, and freighters coming and going from the dock near the city center. Noise from the busy port was muted by large palaces and warehouses along the waterfront.

Castello di Panigai, villa of Contessa Giaiello Ovia

With cool, refreshing air coming off the sea, it was an ideal place for sitting and relaxing. Each evening, the sun set across the sea and the everchanging beautiful colors, clouds, and shadows entertained them until the beautiful night lights lit up the city and harbor below. Anna felt relaxed and peaceful whenever she visited this home.

Not far from her apartment in Pordenone, Anna knew of an artist named, Gioiella Ovio, who was a countess, and lived in Castello di Panigai, Gioiella was an exquisite artist who painted miniature scenes on antique glass bottles. She lived there with Sergio, a professional chef, and her mother, Natalia.

Contessas Gioiella and Graziana Ovio

Allyson was also an artist, so Anna invited her to meet Gioiella at the Castello. Anna was delighted to have made that introduction because Gioiella invited Allyson back to her studio to teach her how to paint on glass. Allyson gave Anna the first bottle she ever painted which featured a juniper tree and Anna kept this little bottle in a place where she could look at it daily as the two women had become deep and lasting friends.

***

After 29 years working for the Americans, Anna retired in 1983, at age 61. It was a bittersweet decision since she didn't want to give up her association with the American base. However, she decided to live a slower-paced life, so after selling her apartment in Pordenone along with much of her furniture, she returned to Trieste to live full time with her cousin, Mario. She also decided to sell her family home in Visco but kept a few paintings and some antique carpets from her mother's side of the family which she returned to their original home in Trieste on via Trenovia. She sold her home in Visco to the Tassins, a wonderful couple who had children and who were college professors in Gorizia. She was happy to see her home occupied by such intelligent and caring people.

Anna moved into her *Zia* Jetti's bedroom, where she had been staying on weekends before she retired. Now she and Mario shared a large parlor, small kitchen, and a dining room on the main floor of the house. She brought with her the little red kitchen cabinets that she had designed in 1957, from her Pordenone apartment, and set up a guest suite downstairs on the ground floor.

The guest suite had double patio doors opening onto the gardens in front of the house where blooming rose bushes and flowers lined the pathways in the garden. A fence was covered with ivy and morning glories. There were large bushes of lilacs in corners of the garden and pots of geraniums framing the doorways and patio. Flowering fruit trees were in a row alongside the garden, and it looked like paradise.

Domingo and Elena Sylos were elderly neighbors who had been friends with Anna and her family for many years. Anna was often invited for afternoon tea in their beautiful garden. Anna started tutoring different languages parttime and soon some of her pupils were Italian school children learning English and French for the first time. Other pupils were adult businessmen or elderly people who already knew other languages and just wanted to practice their conversational skills. One of her favorite pupils was Renata Stock, a wealthy Italian heiress who had a beautiful villa and expansive garden which Anna would visit each week for conversational English lessons. Anna especially enjoyed the opportunity to practice English because it brought her closer to memories of the years she spent in the company of Americans at Aviano Air Force Base.

Anna and Mario complemented one another and entered a period of peaceful and satisfying co-existence. They both enjoyed an active life of gardening, swimming, and walking on the many paths around Trieste. Frequently, they entertained visitors, relatives, and friends.

Anna was delighted when Allyson and her son, Espen, came to visit her from the United States in August 1984. They stayed for nearly a month. Espen was only three years old, so they took him to city parks and to the beach to play. It was wonderful for Anna and Allyson to reconnect and reminisce about their years together at Aviano and to catch up on events in each other's lives.

Later that same year, in November 1984, Mario suddenly died of a heart attack. He left the house and all his belongings to Anna. She continued to live there alone peacefully gardening, visiting friends, and traveling.

She had an open invitation for lunch with her long-time friends, Mafalda and Gianni, whom she had known since the 1950's when she and Gianni had worked together for the Italian government in Trieste. The three of them often took day trips into the country to buy produce and wine.

Even though Anna had a deep attachment to her house and gardens, in 1996, Anna decided to sell her property because it was now too large for her to keep up and manage by herself. The Gelletti family, who bought the house, became Anna's dear friends and invited her to visit the house whenever she wanted. Having this lovely family buy the house made it easier for her to give it up. This house had been a part of her life for over seventy years, and she was leaving it in caring, gentle hands.

Anna bought a small apartment in downtown Trieste on Via Udine near the train station. It was centrally located on major bus lines and within easy walking distance to several good markets, and a nice chapel nearby. She was quietly winding her life down.

Mafalda and Gianni Poropat
Anna's lifelong friends from Trieste

Allyson and Anna Maria
2003

Last picture taken in Trieste
before moving to Rome
2003

Chapter 17
From Allyson

*T**his book is the result of countless stories*, pictures, and telephone conversations made between Anna and myself to clarify events presented in this book. I often traveled to Italy with family and friends from my home in Eau Claire, Wisconsin, where we had moved in 1996. Anna would join us on our adventures to explore different parts of Italy. She was somewhat of an authority on history and art. In 1999, she began traveling to Wisconsin to stay with us for several months at a time. She was able to experience every season there, but the holidays of Thanksgiving and Christmas were her favorite. During her visits, we took mini vacations to different parts of the United States.

In 2002, on Anna's 80th birthday, she flew from Trieste to Toulouse, France, to meet me where we attended a ten-day painting workshop in Sorèze, France. It the first time she had painted and loved it immensely. After the workshop, I rented a car, and we went on a driving tour to Carcassone and surrounding areas. One of our favorite towns was Saint Felix-Lauragais where Anna ordered a handmade tailored suit in French blue.

The following year Anna began to experience constant troubles at her apartment building. Extensive construction was needed on the outside of the building, and updates were needed inside of the complex as well. She did not like many of her neighbors, and none of the apartment owners seemed to agree on which projects were necessary. They were constantly arguing over costs and final decisions could never be made.

Finally, Anna decided she needed to change her environment and be rid of these complications that weighed so heavily on her, mentally, physically and financially. At this time, she also began to develop severe back pain and leg cramps and suspected these were brought on mostly by stress, so she decided to move.

Several years earlier, we had visited a nicely located resident villa in Rome managed by nuns. When we were there, she had talked to them about one day returning as a resident. So, she contacted them again at the Instituto Delle Suore Carmelitane on Via Trionfale and they agreed to rent her a room which included meals. It was located on the hill above the Vatican in an area called Monte Mario.

**The resident villa managed by the
Suore Carmelitane on via Trionfale, Rome
where Anna lived 2003-2004**

She began making arrangements to leave Trieste which bewildered her friends, who were sad to see her move so far away. After placing her apartment on the market, it soon sold; she also sold her car to a friend. I returned to Trieste in September of 2003 to help her pack and close out her apartment and rented a car in Venice for the trip to Rome. We donated clothing and books to her church which we delivered ourselves, and also gave some items to her friends. An antique dealer came to pick up her furniture and carpets to sell on consignment.

She had stacks of things she wanted me to carry to the garbage bin. In that stack, I found many nice photos from Anna's life. When I suggested she keep them, she said, "Throw them away; they are all dead anyway." That saddened me so much, I asked her if I could keep some of them. Later, I used them to help me write her story.

As we left Trieste with all her possessions packed into the car, it was hard to imagine Anna living anywhere else except Trieste. Louis Armstrong's "What a Wonderful World" was playing on the radio. We laughed and sang along. We stopped to visit friends along the way south towards Rome. In Visco we went back to the house she was born in to visit Ferruccio Tassin and family. Also, in Visco, we spent the afternoon visiting Elda and the Simeon family. Elda was a longtime friend of Anna and her family. She was an extraordinary seamstress who had made many of Anna's tailored suits and furs.

Anna was genuinely happy to be going to Rome, relieved of her possessions and troubles involved with owning property. She said she felt lighthearted and was looking forward to living a quiet, simple life with the nuns at Suore Carmelitane Villa, on via Trionfale. After she was settled, she began leisurely exploring Rome, visiting art galleries and monuments. Later, she wrote beautiful letters with little drawings to tell me where she had been and what she had seen.

One day a stray dog took up residence with the sisters and Anna enjoyed caring for him and taking him on daily walks.

There was a caretaker named Oswaldo, a former opera singer, who helped care for the nuns' property and was also the chauffeur for the sisters. He often entertained them by singing and joking with expressions of his love and emotions. All the residents enjoyed his happy enthusiasm. He was also a resident and they shared meals in the dining room, where he often sang till meals were served.

That December, Anna arrived at my home in Wisconsin for several months. We began writing her story using the photos I had saved from the refuse bin in Trieste, as our guide.

Making pizza at the Hansen's home
Wisconsin 2004

The following April, my husband, Jahn, and I went to Rome to visit Anna. We met Jahn's brother, Egil, and his friend, Tove, both from Demark, at Anna's residence in the villa. We spent several days in Rome before taking the train to Florence where we stayed for several days. After Egil and Tove returned to Demark, Jahn rented a car and the three of us drove around

Tuscany and Umbria, spending several days in Perugia. Anna's childhood friend, Maria Tei, had a nice villa on the outskirts of Perugia, so we went to visit Maria and her daughter, Frederica. We all felt a little nostalgic about being in Perugia together again, after 25 years.

Perugia is where Jahn and I met. Indirectly, I guess, Anna was the reason I met him. It was Anna's suggestion back in 1979, that I go to Perugia, because my paintings reminded her of the area. So, I spent over a year in Perugia painting and studying at the International Montessori Teacher's Training Center. Anna made several trips to Perugia during my time there to visit Maria and me. She also attended my graduation ceremony the following year with two of her best friends from northern Italy, Hilda and Mafalda. That is when everyone met Jahn, my future husband, for the first time. Jahn had been living in Perugia for six months studying Italian and Premedical Terminology when we met.

After we took Anna back to Rome, we returned to Wisconsin. That fall, Anna said she was having difficulty finding medical care in Rome because she had not been employed there and had to pay extra. Also, the cost of living in Rome was higher than she had anticipated. So, in November 2004, after having lived in Rome for one year, and after much encouragement from her friends in Trieste, Anna made plans to return to Trieste. She told me: "My Roman holiday has come to an end."

I returned to Rome, rented a car, and again helped Anna move back to Trieste. We took our time touring central Italy on our way northward to Trieste, taking back roads and driving through small villages and spent one night in Assisi, a place we had visited several times, and was dear to us both.

Anna had arranged to rent a small apartment on Via Rossetti near her friends, Mafalda, and Gianni. Arriving in Trieste, we were met by Nereo and Loredanna Vittussi, Anna's new landlords and neighbors. They were helpful and kind and they would become a great source of comfort and support for Anna.

The following April in 2005, Anna arrived at our farm in Wisconsin for a three-month stay. She adored Pippi, a new addition to our family. Pippi was a tiny black toy poodle and smaller than our two cats. While she was with us that summer, Anna was also able to see the birth of my daughter's foal, Achilles, whom she called *Tesoro,* which means "treasure" in Italian.

In early July, we were invited to my niece's wedding in West Virginia. After the celebration, we continued through the mountains of West Virginia and into Maryland where I grew up. Anna had the opportunity to meet the rest of my family and reacquaint herself with my two sisters, Renata, whom she had met in Italy in 1977, and Sherrie, who had accompanied me to Italy with a friend in 1998. Then we returned to Wisconsin for a couple more weeks.

Anna's tourist visa to the U.S. was good through the twenty-third of July. So, after we celebrated my birthday, our daughter Kate and I accompanied Anna back to Italy. We spent three glorious weeks visiting friends in Trieste, Asolo, Ravenna, Perugia, Florence, San Gimignano, and Parma.

On our way back north to Trieste, we stopped to visit our friend, Gioiella, at Castello di Panagia. The last time Anna, Kate and I had seen Gioiella was in 2001 when we had visited with my son, Espen, Kate, and my two cousins, Dan, and Jane. Gioiella invited neighborhood friends, Mario and Robin Radice, and their daughter, Liberty, for a wonderful lunch in her grand dining room, which the Germans had occupied during WWII. Gioiella had first met Espen when he was only three years old in 1984. She had set him up in a beautiful little iron framed bed that she had used as a baby. It was wonderful to be all together again in that magnificent villa.

Then we returned to Trieste for a few days and decided to go to Venice for the last four days of our trip. I hadn't been to Venice with Anna since the 1970's when we used to go there to have her shoes made. She had such tiny feet that it was hard for her to find shoes small enough. This time, we stayed in Hotel Flora on the Grand Canal near St. Mark's Square. Anna retraced some of the streets and areas where she and Giorgio had been together years ago when he was a student at Ca' Foscari University.

That Sunday, we attended Mass at St. Mark's Cathedral entering by the side door because the main entrance was roped off for tourists who were lining up. Each evening we went to St. Mark's square to watch people passing by. When the orchestras started playing, we took our seats, sipping on drinks and eating gelato. At one point Anna stood up and danced a little, laughing the whole time. Kate played with the pigeons and joined us from time to time, as we sat in the cool night air until the orchestra stopped playing around 11:00 p.m. We all agreed life was indeed sweet, and that memories are one of the most precious possessions any person can have.

On the last day in Venice, Kate and I accompanied Anna to the train station in Mestre where she continued on to Trieste, while Kate and I caught the bus to Aeroporto Marco Polo. We boarded a plane and returned home. Our four-month trip of being together with Anna was over.

The following year, Anna did not feel well enough to visit us in the spring as she had planned. She began experiencing a great amount of pain in her stomach area and felt weak and tired much of the time. She went to numerous doctors throughout the spring and summer. Then after many tests and an exploratory surgery, it was determined she had developed inoperable pancreatic cancer.

I flew to Trieste to be with her when she went to the Casa di Cure in Aurisina, a nursing facility on the outskirts of Trieste, for hospice care. I stayed alone in her apartment but made daily trips to spend time with her. Many of her friends also came to visit for a while. After one week, Anna told the staff at Aurisina that she was feeling better and wanted me to take her home. They released her into my care, and I drove her home the long way along the coast so we could watch the sun setting on the water. That evening after a small meal, we made jokes and laughed late into the night.

I could see Anna had lost much weight and wasn't stable on her feet any longer. However, for an eighty-four-year-old woman, her mind was extremely sharp. She arranged for several people to come to her apartment and help her when I had to return home.

The following month our son, Espen, was in the military and stationed in Iraq. He had a two-week leave so I flew back to Italy to meet him in Venice so we could go see Anna together. She was overjoyed to see Espen again. We had a wonderful visit, and I am glad Espen was with me when I left her apartment for what I suspected would be the last time. She followed us into the hall and waved, blowing kisses as the elevator doors closed.

On December 30, 2006, Anna became too weak to continue living alone. She was admitted into a clinic in downtown Trieste and told me not worry, that she was not afraid of death because she believed in God and His promise of eternal life with Him.

From her window at the clinic, she could look up the hill and see her grandparent's house on Via Trenovia. I called her each day to give her an update of Pippi's activities, and let her know how wonderfully brave she was, and how much I loved her.

**Anna boarding the train for Trieste
from Mestre Train Station**

Anna passed away on February 10, 2007. Her friends said that the last time she spoke, she called my name. She was cremated and her ashes returned to the cemetery in Visco, where Elda lovingly cares for her grave. Anna is still missed, loved, and remembered by those who knew her and her wonderful spirit.

ANNA MARIA VENTURINI

ABOUT THE AUTHOR

Alice (Allyson) Hansen grew up on a farm in western Maryland. Upon graduating from high school, she joined the U.S. Air Force and was eventually stationed as the first single female airman (WAF) at Aviano Air Force Base in Aviano, Italy.

There she met Anna Maria Venturini, an Italian secretary for the office, and they became lifelong friends.

Anna introduced Allyson to the Italian lifestyle, language, history, and customs.

After an honorable discharge from the military, Allyson returned to Italy to live and work in Perugia where she attended the A.M.I. Montessori Training Course for one year, graduating in April 1980. She then worked in Venice as an early staff member for the establishment of the Peggy Guggenheim Collection at Palazzo Vanier Dei Leoni on the Grand Canal.

In 1981, Allyson married Jahn Hansen. Both were students and had met during her year in Perugia. Then they moved to his native Norway. Two years later, they decided to move the United States to pursue a higher education. They raised two children and have three grandchildren.

Anna became an adopted member of the Hansen family and often came to visit for extended periods on their farm in Wisconsin. Over the years, Allyson continued to make frequent trips to Italy, visiting Anna and her friends in Trieste.

To this day, she continues her love of "all things Italian" and currently lives in Florida with her wonderful memories of travels with Anna Maria Venturini.

Made in the USA
Columbia, SC
22 June 2023